PLAYW

FROM PAGI

PLAYWRITING
FROM PAGE TO STAGE

Christopher William Hill

ROBERT HALE · LONDON

ISBN 978-0-7090-9099-1

Robert Hale Limited
Clerkenwell House
Clerkenwell Green
London EC1R 0HT

www.halebooks.com

A catalogue record for this book is available from the British Library

2 4 6 8 10 9 7 5 3 1

Typeset by e-type, Liverpool
Printed in Great Britain by the MPG Books Group,
Bodmin and King's Lynn

For Dad: who doesn't want to become
a playwright, so will never read this.

<u>WARNING!</u>

'Playwright' is a good, solid word. Like wheelwright or shipwright. Playwriting is about craft every bit as much as it is about art. If you want the Muse to drop round and deliver an idea into your hands, then this book probably isn't for you. Occasionally people will treat playwrights as demi-gods, who channel energy from some unseen and unknowable force. They are not and do not.

This book doesn't have the power to turn you into a playwright. *No* book can transform you into a playwright. Only you have that power. Now read on …

How to use this book

This book is designed for inexperienced playwrights, as well as more experienced writers. Feel free to scribble all over the book (unless you've borrowed it from the library). Slip it in your bag. Take it with you on your way to work. Think of this as a friend in book form. Dip in and out; this is a workbook after all.

There's no magic formula to becoming a successful playwright. I'd be inclined to say there aren't secrets, but there are certainly some proven truths.

Getting started

You don't need any qualifications or specific training to become a playwright. Theoretically, anybody could pick up a pen and devote the rest of their life to writing plays. In thousands and thousands of rooms around the world, other writers are going through exactly the same thing as you. And I'll be honest, there are easier jobs you could be doing. But I'm assuming you may well be reading this book because you're not all that interested in easy jobs.

I'm also making certain assumptions about you as a writer. First, I'm assuming that you have a place that you can go to write. Second, I'm assuming you have access to a computer. And third, unlike poetry or prose, it's my belief that very few people write plays for purely recreational purposes. What would be the point? So I'm also assuming that you're interested in writing professionally.

Writing a play is a process

I notice that in this book I use the word 'process' a lot – and there's an important reason for this. Playwriting is a process (there I go again); a script rarely springs into fruition. An idea germinates in a writer's mind and is then translated on to the page – it's as simple or as complicated as that.

But while there is a process, I don't think there's any *system* for writing plays. In fact, I think it's the suspicion that there might be a system that puts many potentially talented writers off the idea of writing plays. So use what's useful for you in this book, ignore what isn't.

Think of this as the holistic approach to playwriting. Writing the play is just a tiny part of the job. If this book can go some way towards demystifying the process of writing a play, then it will have achieved its goal.

> 'The structure of a play is always the story of how the birds came home to roost.'
>
> *Arthur Miller*

We all have that ongoing internal voice that we often have to silence, for the sake of our own sanity. The voice that says: 'What makes you think anyone's ever going to be interested in what you have to say?'

Be honest with yourself. Don't allow false modesty to get in the way. The fact that you picked up this book and started reading is a sure sign that, no matter how deep down, you believe you have stories that are worth telling. And if your stories are worth telling, they almost certainly need an audience. Have confidence in your own arrogance. If you didn't think you could write a play, you wouldn't be writing one. You probably wouldn't even be reading these words right now.

So what exactly is it like to be a playwright? Well, what is it like to be any other sort of human being? Playwrights come in a variety of different shapes and sizes. Their politics may be left wing, right wing or somewhere in the middle. They might be people you'd like to sit down and have a chat with; they might not. In short, playwrights can be people like you and me.

Don't be too academic

When I was applying for a drama degree course, I went for an interview with an American academic. He asked me why

I wanted to study drama. 'I want to be a playwright,' I said. 'I think studying plays will help me with that.' He looked at me doubtfully, and politely told me I was wrong. And in a way, he was right to do so. An overly academic approach to playwriting can get in the way of producing a script.

Don't expect to *feel* a certain way as you write your play

Possibly you're feeling rather daunted by the prospect of writing a play. But it's natural to be scared, isn't it? Whatever you're feeling now, every writer will have experienced at some point in his or her career. Minimize the pressure to 'succeed'. Why is it that all those people who endlessly drone on about the book they're going to write never write it? Simple, it's because they've raised unrealistic expectations by telling everybody all about it. Keep the play you're writing a secret – and keep this secret under wraps until it's ready to be seen. There's something unfortunately cathartic about sharing your idea with too many people. And there's an easy solution to this – don't tell anyone.

'The play's the thing,' wrote William Shakespeare – and he was bang on the money.

So here's your first question:

Why do you want to write plays?

Why write a play? Have you ever asked yourself that question? If your answer is 'Because I wanted to write screenplays and TV scripts, but I think theatre might be easier,' then I strongly advise you to stop and reconsider.

The opportunities that theatre provides are so incredible that it's frustrating when some people see it as an apprenticeship before working in TV or film. It is what it is – embrace the medium.

Flick through the index of any 'Get Rich Quick' manual and I defy you to find playwriting listed anywhere. Very few people turn to playwriting solely for financial gain and there's a reason for this. So – do you want to be rich or do you want to be a writer?

I would be lying if I told you that nobody ever made their fortune writing plays. I can think of several writers who became millionaires almost overnight. But chances are you may never become one of those gilded few. There will almost always be easier ways to earn a living.

First things first

'I don't wait for inspiration. I'm not, in fact, quite sure what inspiration is, but I'm sure that if it is going to turn up, my having started work is the pre-condition of its arrival.'

Quentin Blake

The Russian theatre director Constantin Stanislavski said something very wise and inspirational: 'Start bravely, not to reason, but to act.' I think we can misquote him here. 'Start bravely, not to reason, but to write.' If you're waiting for a nirvana-like state of being, you'll never write a single word.

What is the worst that can happen if you put pen to page? It's not about right or wrong at this stage. It's simply a chance to experiment. Think of all the brilliant plays that could have been written if writers had not procrastinated. A good friend of mine has been on the verge of writing a very good one for a number of years, but I'm not entirely sure that it will ever be finished.

So here's a tip. Allow yourself the freedom to write (even if it's wrong), knowing that absolutely nothing is written in stone.

Tell a taxi driver you're a playwright and they'll always pity you ...

Taxi driver: So what do you do?
Playwright: What do I do?
Taxi driver: For a living.
Playwright: Right. I'm a playwright.
Taxi driver: For the telly?
Playwright: No, theatre really.
Taxi driver: Don't worry, mate. You'll see your name up on the telly one day.

Or even more dispiritingly:

Taxi driver: I had that Pinter bloke in the back of my cab once.

You're at a party with a plate of cocktail nibbles and a glass of bubbly. You don't know anybody, so you engage in stilted conversation with the first poor soul you bump into:

'So. What do you do?'
'Oh, I'm a playwright.'

'Really? Have you written any plays I might have heard
   of?'
'I haven't actually *written* a play yet.'

This, my friend, is a dilettante. A dabbling amateur. Pick
up your glass of cava and plate of Twiglets and quickly
move as far away from this person as possible. They will
never write a play. What's more, they have no *intention* of
writing a play. They are labouring under the misapprehen-
sion that 'I think I want to be, therefore I am'. In most jobs
you have to attain a certain level of competence before you
can confidently pass yourself off as, say, a cordon bleu chef,
physicist or surgeon:

'So. What do you do?'
'Oh, I'm a brain surgeon.'
'Really? Have you operated on anybody I might have
   heard of?'
'I haven't actually *operated* on anybody yet.'

See? You'd never have *that* conversation (but if you ever
do, move quicker and even further away. Drop the cava and
Twiglets – it's collateral damage).

Build a library of playwriting books

There are books that talk you through practically every
aspect of the craft and it's well worth building up a collection of the books which feel instinctively right for you. This
has always got to be a question of personal taste.

Some 'self-help' books bully writers into believing there
is only one path to follow, and that path must be followed

with no deviation whatsoever from the laboriously pre-scribed route (no nipping off to pick the flowers on the way to Grandma's house). My feeling about this is simple: twaddle. If it's mind-numbingly difficult and makes your brain hurt, it's probably not helping.

I'm also rather suspicious of anyone who comes up with a system for writing plays. I don't have a scientific or mathematical bone in my body, and any tome that's laid out like out a pie chart or periodic table fills me with a sense of despair.

Sometimes writers become slaves to prescriptive exer-cises. Often these exercises can be an invaluable way of fine-tuning aspects of your writing process, but I do think they have the potential to get in the way. Think of playwrit-ing as a recipe. Now, I'm an enthusiastic cake baker. If I'm told I've got to whisk the mixture, fair enough. If I'm told *how* to whisk the mixture I rapidly lose interest. It gets in the way of the recipe (in moments of doubt I fall back pretty heavily on culinary analogies).

Use playwriting exercises as and when you think they're necessary – but don't become a martyr to them. Remember, a writing exercise can only take you so far and is never a replacement for the act of sitting down and getting on with your play. I'm a great believer in learning as you go. As you begin writing a play, your knowledge will grow rapidly and exponentially.

So what exactly are we trying to achieve when we sit down to write a play? At the most basic level, we're telling a story. No matter how abstract or disjointed the style, the audience will be taken on a journey. You start at point A (the opening line of your play) and stop at point B (the final line, on the final page of your script). These are givens.

So imagine an entirely empty stage. The lights are raised. An actor bounds slowly onto this empty space:

Astronaut 1: Houston, this is Marvin. I'm standing on the moon's surface.

As an audience, we've got no reason to doubt his word. We're willing to suspend disbelief. On this empty stage a character has entered and given us a hint. Perhaps a second actor enters:

Astronaut 2: It's big, isn't it?
Astronaut 1: What is?
Astronaut 2: This. The moon.

So, to all intents and purposes, we know where we are. This is a lunar mission. We're standing on the surface of the moon – unless something happens to puncture this 'reality' …

Woman enters, observes Astronaut 1 suspiciously.
Woman: Excuse me? Do you know if this is the stop for No. 28?

People often sit down and start writing what they think a play *should be.* And it's often based on a rather shaky and outdated understanding of what theatre should be. So here's a thought that might free up your thinking a bit:

Theatre can be whatever you *want* it to be.

Honestly, it really can.

Where do ideas come from? How can I get some?

If you're asking this question, then maybe playwriting isn't the job for you. There's a basic misconception that play ideas arrive fully formed. They don't.

Ideas are forming all the time; we've just got to be open to that particular process. You have to be magpie-like in your acquisitiveness, grabbing information whenever and wherever you can. I remember going to a funeral once. At the wake, over tea and saffron cake, I heard a relative telling a story: 'There was a homosexual, a Pole and a skiffle group...'

As far as I remember, none of them ended happily. The inanity of the conversations, juxtaposed with the enormity of death, seemed to offer a host of dramatic possibilities. Fragments of overheard conversation like this can quickly add up to something more substantial. But people are often quick to dismiss ideas: 'It's probably stupid. And anyway, I don't know how it ends.'

Why should you know how it ends? Again, coming up with an idea for a play is a *process*. It seems that for many people if the idea doesn't hit them fully formed, it's dismissed as weak and lacking in potential. A lot of the time this really isn't true. An idea will often build up incrementally, so allow time for your thoughts to simmer. And be prepared for a long wait. Sometimes it's taken years for an idea to germinate and become the basis of a play. Do as I do and live by the maxim 'all in good time'. Don't expect everything to fall into place overnight. Rest assured – the play will take as long as it takes.

'Only connect.'
E.M. Forster

Why go to the theatre anyway?

It's difficult for some writers to get their heads round the idea that people don't always go to the theatre as a form of ritualized self-abuse. It never occurs to them that an audience might actually like to have a good time. Too many people seem to think that the theatre is a worthy institution, a place we attend for moral improvement.

Theatre can embrace the misery and the joy of the world. And what's more, it can embrace misery and joy in the same play. Life is absurd, and the best plays reflect this. Your audience will be spending a couple of hours sitting in the dark. Do them a favour. Give them two hours to enjoy. It shouldn't be theatre's responsibility to prove that life really is too short.

Unless you try to entertain your audience, chances are they'll stop listening to whatever you have to say. There's a wonderful quote, anonymous I think, which serves as a gentle reminder to all writers:

> 'An audience will forgive you practically anything, except boring them.'

The well-made play

Many right-minded people use 'the well-made play' as a pejorative term. But what's wrong with a play that has a clearly demarked beginning, middle and end?

I'm convinced that we have an innate understanding of a basic three-act structure, with a beginning, a middle and an end. An audience will always want a good story well told. How you choose to set about doing this is completely up to you. There is never a definitive way of doing anything.

Everything means something

This is *your* world. And in this world nothing occurs purely by chance. There is a god, and you are it. From your position on high, gazing down on your creations, the word 'accident' is a meaningless concept. There is no such thing as 'free will' on your newly-created planet – every word spoken, every action performed, is a direct consequence of *your* imagination. And there is something supremely satisfying about ordering this world.

Six simple rules for playwrights

1 You're more likely to write your play if you're sitting at your desk than if you're not.
2 Don't expect to get everything right immediately.
3 If you can't get it right, get it written.
4 Live life – it can only enrich your writing.
5 Do remember to eat.
6 Don't give up if you fall at the first fence. A lot of very promising playwrights simply give up too early. Dealing with rejection is part and parcel of the job.

Are monologues cheating? Is it a lazy way of getting information across?

'Narrators should not be necessary: in a play the story is unfolded through the dialogue.'

This was a note from my sage English teacher, Mr Godolphin, marking a script I wrote at the tender age of twelve. He also wrote, 'There is no need for speech marks when you have names in the margin.' Words to live by. Remember, you're not writing a novel. Your script doesn't need a narrator to provide the narrative – that's the job of the dialogue.

I would always urge caution with monologues. Or to put it another way: 'Is your monologue really necessary?'

Monologues are often used lazily as a vehicle for conveying information quickly. In almost every case you can get this information across through dialogue.

We're not used to being talked *at* any more. Apart from anything else, it's far more difficult to digest information in solid chunks. Monologues can provide an opportunity for your character to articulate all the thoughts they might otherwise keep under wraps, revealing their innermost feelings and desires. But of course, we don't always *want* an explicit understanding of the innermost workings of a character's mind. Often, we want to work that out for ourselves – reading between lines of dialogue to work out the unspoken subtext. This is almost always the most dramatically satisfying approach.

So what's the difference between conversation and dramatic dialogue?

OK, so here's an exercise. Tape an 'overheard' conversation and write an accurate transcript. Be strict with yourself, paying close attention to pauses, interruptions and overlaps.

Read back through this transcript and chart the flow of the conversation. People interrupt and overlap, their conversation twists and meanders, it gains speed, then loses momentum. In terms of texture this is undoubtedly interesting, but is it dramatic? Well, in most cases no.

Dialogue is conversation with a *purpose* – it has a dramatic imperative. Or to put it another way, dialogue is *dramatically motivated* speech. There needs to be a spark of conflict underlying the dialogue. What you don't want is dialogue that drifts listlessly. Too often characters come on stage for an idle natter. No one cares about inconsequential gossiping – you have to earn your stage time.

Ask yourself the question, 'What is the dramatic imperative that will underpin my play?' *Why* have I chosen to tell the story on stage? *Why* have I chosen to tell the story at all?

Strip the story back to its basics. If you were going to sum up the idea for your play in a single sentence, what would it be? You have chosen this slice of your characters' lives for a reason. And the reason is this:

It's the slice of their lives when something really interesting happens.

If this statement doesn't seem accurate, stop to consider why not. It's all a question of jeopardy and stakes: 'What's the jeopardy?' and 'Are the stakes high enough?'

Imagine you're viewing your play as a graph. We want to see pleasing peaks and troughs of dramatic tension. Each and every scene should be driven by an underlying sense of conflict.

Is it true you should only 'write what you know'?

Did Harold Pinter work as a caretaker? Well, no. Can a play about an axe murderer only be written by an axe murderer? Of course not. Does a career as a playwright only leave a dramatist fit to write plays about playwriting? What a dull world that would be. So let's not take the exhortation at face value, or there's a danger that you're only ever going to write one type of character – you.

'I draw from life – but I always pulp my acquaintance before serving them up. You would never recognize a pig in a sausage.'

Frances Trollope

Mrs Trollope (Anthony's mother) knew a thing or two. In most cases, the characters we create are a mishmash of many, many different people. It's rarely as easy as picking a character you know in 'real life' and dropping them on to the page. They undergo a process of metamorphosis. A character is most likely an amalgam of personality traits drawn from a number of people you know, bound together by your creative imagination. It reminds me of the creation of dinosaurs in *Jurassic Park* – adding frog DNA to complete the genetic code. Your imagination, for the purpose of this argument, is the frog DNA.

A playwright is a conduit, taking in information through a process of osmosis, and slowly converting it into drama. In some way, shape or form, a dramatist's work is a reaction to the world they see around them – no matter how strange or obscure the play, whether it's contemporary, historical or even futuristic.

What you see is not what you get

Don't be afraid to make your characters complicated. I don't believe a character without flaws actually exists. Do you know any entirely uncomplicated people? I don't. And if you think you do, I can only assume you don't know them as well as you think you do.

So here's a question: 'Are your characters always telling the truth?'

In 'real life' we only reveal as much or as little as we choose. We rarely tell all, and what we do tell isn't always accurate – because we're trying to protect someone's feelings, or our opinion is clouded by subjectivity, or it's a downright lie.

The all-important character 'hole'

What holds you back in life and prevents you from fulfilling your potential? For me, it's probably hypochondria and a slight tendency towards Obsessive Compulsive Disorder. Normally I have it under control. Or if not exactly under control, I've developed strategies to disguise it. I'm a functioning Obsessive Compulsive.

I was giving a talk in Brazil, and looked in my bag to try and find props to help illustrate the kind of person I am. I was awash with indigestion tablets, Rescue Remedy spray and a TAM in-flight sick bag (in case of emergency). If I'm tired or under pressure (a looming deadline, for example), then right on cue the Obsessive Compulsive Disorder kicks in (I mentioned this in a playwriting workshop once and one of the participants was convinced his wife could cure me). You should see me with a light switch – it's a joy. On, off, on, off ... on. So that's one of my 'character holes'.

But does this sound dramatic to you? Is there potential for dramatic conflict here?

Well, probably. Let's call our hypochondriac Character A, and his long-suffering mother Character B. Every time Character

A visits Character B, he complains about the nagging head-ache which would seem to suggest the presence of brain lesions, or the persistent ache in his hip which may be some rare and hitherto undiagnosed form of cancer. Character B has undoubtedly grown heartily sick of this never-ending roll call of symptoms, and who can blame her? So there's clearly some potential for conflict there. What else can we throw into the mix? Suppose Character B is actually dying, but hasn't told Character A. See how that might complicate things?

> Nina: Your play is hard to act, there are no living people in it.
>
> Treplev: Living people! We should show life neither as it is nor as it ought to be, but as we see it in our dreams.

> *Anton Chekhov*

It's your right to eavesdrop

I'd go further – it's your *duty* to listen in on conversations. There's a potential treasure-trove of characters out there waiting to be overheard. We've all listened in to conversations (go on, admit it, you do really) – snatches of lives overheard on buses, in restaurants, outside the local super-market. Think about how much of a life you can imagine from these snippets of conversation – these little vignettes.

Recently I was waiting on a railway platform. Two teenage girls were standing close to me, off for a day out at the beach. One of the girls commented that it was 'lush' to have got up at six in the morning, as it was just getting light. She started to play with her friend's hair.

> Girl 1: It's cute. It's a bit manic, but it's cute.

w, to me this is a gift of a line. Little is said but much is
ealed. Instantly we can start to make leaps of faith and a
character begins to assert itself. Girl 1 takes the lead; she
voices her opinions and believes Girl 2 is happy to go along
with them. Assuming they spend all day on the beach
together, will the relationship become more strained? Will
Girl 2 rebel against her friend? The cogs start to whirr and
two characters slowly take shape.

There was a woman I overheard in a gift shop in
Chelmsford, desperately hunting out a present for a friend:

> **Woman:** I could buy her one of those Jesus candles. She
> likes Jesus.

Incredible, you couldn't make it up. And then there was the
woman I overheard in Debenhams, clutching an enormous
ceramic cupcake in her arms:

> **Woman:** That's why I couldn't find it online. I spelt
> cupcake wrong.

I think of it as Fate offering a helping hand. I hardly ever
leave home without a notebook and pen; you never know
when you might hear something useful. Often something
that's fascinating in the moment has no obvious practical
application, and then on occasions you strike a little
nugget, a tiny piece of a life that can inform an entire play.
In the 1990s I heard an Irish drunk on the streets of
Canterbury:

> **Man:** I used to be a writer, but I lost my Olivetti.

A diary with a difference ...

Keep a journal, it'll help you to track the genesis and development of your play. An idea for a play rarely drops from the heavens fully formed. We piece it together, little by little. You may have read a magazine article, overheard a snatch of conversation – slowly these disparate threads get drawn together. Commit everything you can to paper!

The naming of parts

The name of a character can instantly betray a number of facts – everything from nationality to age or 'class'. Think about how names become adapted. Emma can become Em, or Emmie to her closest friends. Also think about how names influence nicknames.

The telephone directory is also well worth a look when you're choosing character names. For foreign names the internet can be a mine of knowledge, with many sites focusing on country-specific surnames and christian names. There are a number of names I'm dying to work into a play at some point. I once knew a Kneebone at school. Have you ever heard of a character called Kneebone? Neither have I. Who could this mythical 'Kneebone' be? A butcher? An ironically named osteopath? The mind boggles.

I used to write villains of the playground into my scripts (they never ended happily), certain in the knowledge that the manuscript would be lodged in the British Library and their names would live on in infamy. Then I got over myself.

What does a name say about a character? What exactly are you trying to convey with your character's name? Give time and thought to the naming of your characters; don't just apply the names arbitrarily – it's a wasted opportunity. I always have a book of babies' names to hand and I've started my own useful 'book of names' – scribbling down anything of interest I come across that I think might be useful at a later date.

How do I make sure there's enough conflict in my play?

Don't forget – at the heart of your play you must have a clear dramatic imperative. What's the conflict that underpins your idea?

Sometimes a playwright will submit a script, bursting at the seams with good dialogue. The problem is, there's no drama. Even the best dialogue writers will lose their audience if there's no dramatic engine driving the play forward. It's this conflict that people will be looking out for – this is the mortar that holds the play together.

Obviously, good dialogue is an integral part of the play. But sparkling wit and dialogue are only ever the icing on the cake. Without a satisfying dramatic heart to the play you have nothing.

There are many first plays that are packed full of interesting ideas, but not necessarily *dramatic* ideas. The drama comes in how characters negotiate the obstacles life throws at them, and ultimately whether or not they're successful.

There can be a misguided belief that somehow the 'drama' of the play is an external force. Think of your characters as electrically charged particles. We want to see the sparks fly – a series of little bombs waiting to explode. It's your responsibility to prevent your characters from having an easy ride. Throw as many curve balls as you can. We want things to start going wrong. It's not your job to make your characters' lives easy.

There's no reason at all why your characters can't sort out their problems by the end of the play (the resolution of the conflict). But if the characters get on well throughout the play – where's the drama? Apply the thumbscrews.

A good playwright looks for the worst in people, because that's where the potential for dramatic conflict lies. It's not that we have a particularly jaundiced view of the world, but we do know which side our bread is buttered.

Make sure that each character has their own distinctive voice

We all have our own distinctive speech patterns, conversational tics and specific choices of vocabulary. My sentences are scattered with 'great', 'fantastic' and 'absolutely'. I'm embarrassed by the number of times I start a conversation with 'I mean' or complete a sentence with 'you know what I mean?'

Talking to my sister, a teacher, I sometimes have a nagging suspicion that she's forgotten she's not talking to a nine-year-old. In fairness to my sister, maybe I sometimes behave like a nine-year-old. I do have a nasty habit of finishing my sister's sentences for her – I'm always wrong.

Consider how the following characters might communicate with each other:

a) A couple who've been living together for twenty years.
b) A couple on their first date.
c) A mother and son.
d) A father and daughter.

I love listening to couples who've been together for years – the rhythm of their conversation can be fascinating and revealing. The way the words often tumble across each other.

Remember to continue listening in on conversations. How often do they follow a linear route?

What is an ellipsis and how can it help me?

I'd be surprised if there were many punctuation marks as useful to a playwright as the ellipsis. It shows that the character is trailing off. They've reached the end of a thought. It suggests that the other characters are allowing this trail-off.

Rachel: So maybe I'll go out ...
Tom: Sure.

What the ellipsis is *not* doing here is suggesting that the line is interrupted by another character, jumping in with a new thought. Sometimes a writer uses an ellipsis when they actually mean to use a dash (more on this later).

An ellipsis is also a useful way of suggesting a break in the dialogue. For example, Rachel has answered her mobile, but we only hear Rachel's side of the conversation:

Rachel: Yeah ... yeah ... that's what I said ...

A famous actor once told me that he always asks theatres to remove ellipses before they send on his copy of the script. Sometimes we have to humour actors.

So what's different about a dash?

A dash makes clear that the line is being interrupted.

Rachel: So what I'm thinking is –
Todd: You think I'm having an affair.
Rachel: Don't tell me what I'm thinking.

Pauses

How do you define a pause? Theoretically, I suppose a pause could last as long as you want. In practice, the duration will be defined by the director and actors. Pinter was perhaps the leading proponent of the well-placed pause.

Should I indicate how long a pause lasts?

They pause for thirty seconds.

Try it now. Time a thirty-second pause. A long time, isn't it?

Often pauses are employed lazily. But when a pause is working at its best, it can create a breathtaking effect on stage. Allow pauses to speak. What is left unspoken can often be more electrifying and illuminating than any explicit, articulated thought. What your character doesn't say is another way of helping to tell the story.

What is a beat?

Not to be confused with a story beat (which, in screenwriting, is the term used for a scene-by-scene plot synopsis), a beat is a much more specific break in the action. Beats mean different things to different people. For me, a beat has always been a finger click. It's the break that makes the old 'Why did the chicken cross the road?' gag work.

This works:

Why did the chicken cross the road?

BEAT

To get to the other side.

This *doesn't* work:

Why did the chicken cross the road?

PAUSE

To get to the other side.

This doesn't work too well either:

Why did the chicken cross the road? To get to the other side.

Don't forget your characters!

It can be a bit like spinning plates. Remember who is on stage at any one time. You can get so carried away with an exchange between two characters that you've completely forgotten that a third character has been languishing mutely in the background through ten pages of dialogue. No reason of course why you can't have a silent character – but it might just not be what you'd intended.

Some characters will speak less than other characters. As in life, some people just don't have very much to say – because they're bored, taciturn, inarticulate. But then again, are they coiled like a serpent, ready to strike? Are they sly, watchful, allowing their fellow characters just enough rope to hang themselves?

Some characters naturally hog the limelight. Other characters might prefer to hold back. And then comes the eureka moment when the character finally opens their mouth, and who knows what happens next?

Don't volunteer information too easily

Imagine a parent is looking after a baby. The baby cries.

Baby: Feed me.
Parent: Yes.

Parent feeds Baby.

Let's call this 'what baby wants, baby gets'. Of course, in 'real life', social interaction is a good deal more complicated than this. We're rarely given the response we require.

Baby: Feed me.
Parent: No.

Or, perhaps a step further ...

Baby: Feed me.

Parent turns their back on Baby.

It's the same with characters in plays. They often behave at this elementary level:

Character one: I want information.
Character two: Of course. Here is the information you want.

Rather unsatisfactory, isn't it? This is the problem with spoon-feeding the audience – the more you tell them, the less they have to find out for themselves. And the less they have to find out, the less inclined they'll be to care.

It's not your job to give an audience an easy ride. Make them work.

Don't give your audience too much information

The word 'exposition' is often used in the pejorative sense when it comes to playwriting. The 'exposing' of information is often necessary to help an audience understand a story, but at times it can become obvious that characters are revealing a little too much and then we begin to smell a rat.

> Husband: How long have we been married, Helen? Twelve years, is it? But it only seems like yesterday that we met in Guatemala ...

Of course, there can be benefits to a little bit of expositional writing, especially in the first draft of a script. It can help a writer to make sense of the play he or she is writing. But remember to cut back later on.

Status

Recently, I was talking to a group of writers. And in this group there were four close friends. I asked them to write down who had the highest status. They all wrote down the same name, including the person who believed he had the highest status.

Think about prison pecking order. There's always a need to identify the 'top dog', and this is a position of relative security. It's the 'generals' that are perhaps in a more insecure position, jockeying for pole position. Conversely, for a character with the lowest status, the only way is up.

Imagine you've just arrived at a party. You've said 'hello' to your host, picked up your drink, and been thrust into a room of complete strangers. What do you do? Chances are you take stock before doing anything. It doesn't take us long to get a sense of the pecking order. You work out who is the loudest member of the group but you also work out who the wallflower is – and then you try to place everyone else on this sliding scale. Then you work out where you belong. Are you the shy retiring type who spends the evening talking in hushed tones to the wallflower, or do you feel confident that your stories are more interesting than the raconteur and attempt to compete? We all do it. And sometimes we're right and sometimes we're wrong when we make these snap character judgements, but deep down I'm convinced it's all to do with a primal desire for self-protection. It's every bit as basic as wolves in the arctic tundra deciding whether to lead or be led. And if a wolf incorrectly asserts its authority, it's likely to get bitten.

It's the same with the characters in our plays. Of course, status can be a fluid commodity. A character's stock can slip. A character can also be self-deluded, believing his or her status to be higher or lower than it actually is. This in itself can be a cause of conflict. And conflict is often created by this elementary power struggle, as characters attempt to readjust their places in the pecking order.

Status is not always as obvious as it may initially seem. A character who shouts and screams and throws his or her weight around is not necessarily the highest-status character in a play. In fact, the explicit demonstration of anger may itself be indicative of a lower status. On the other hand, apparently shy and retiring characters with a propensity for passive-aggression can impose their own high status.

Back to school

Cast your mind back to your schooldays. Remember what it was like to write an essay? A question would be posed and your essay would be a response to that question. In your introduction, you'd say what you were going to say. In the main body of your essay, you'd say what you said you were going to say. Then, in your conclusion, you'd say *why* you said what you said you were going to say (and then went on to say!). Without the argument underpinning the essay, your work would have been little more than an abstract collection of thoughts. The argument was the backbone of your essay. A play functions in much the same way.

At its best, theatre is a dynamic, challenging and anarchic force. Unlike a school essay, feel free to pose questions without ever feeling you have to provide all the answers.

Imagine an empty space ...

Imagine a single chair has been placed on an empty stage. An audience will immediately start trying to work out the significance of that chair. Unless we're in for a night of experimental minimalist drama, we're pretty sure that at some point an actor will enter the stage and sit on that chair (or stand on that chair, or lean on that chair, or relate to that chair in some way or other).

Sometimes an audience can be given an inaccurate sense of this stage world before a single word has been spoken. Sometimes this is intentional, sometimes it's not. I was sitting next to a middle-aged couple for a performance of Ibsen's *Rosmersholm*. It was an impressive set, featuring a number of nineteenth-century filing cabinets. The wife leaned over to the husband and whispered: 'Wonderful storage space.'

Where should I set my scene?

Think about the ways in which environment might impact on your characters.

So here's a 'for instance'. The setting is a lounge in a modern flat. A party is in full swing. A woman (let's call her Ally) sits on the sofa, clearly uncomfortable in this environment. A second woman (Tess) is trying to encourage Ally to let her hair down, and get into the party mood. Ally is resistant. A third character enters (Max). Max has been cooking in the kitchen and hasn't realized that Ally's arrived. It becomes clear that Ally hasn't been to the flat in a while – actually this is the first time she's been round since her boyfriend collapsed and died in front of the coffee table.

See what I mean? The choice of location suddenly plays an important part in the structure of the play. Think about how your characters behave in the space, and more importantly *why*.

Wherever possible we want to take characters out of their 'comfort zone' and drop them, kicking and screaming, into a potentially hostile environment.

There's a gladiatorial aspect to all this. I remember as a boy collecting spiders in a jar and watching with grim fascination as one of the arachnids consumed another. As a rule,

I'm sure each of the spiders would have crossed the street to avoid the other, thus preventing this cannibalistic orgy. This is what we're doing as playwrights. The confines of the play are the confines of the glass jar. We're unscrewing the lid and dropping in characters that are destined not to get on – although they may well draw the line at cannibalism.

Finding your characters

Imagine the life of your central character laid out as a vast panoramic sweep of action – a latter-day 'Bayeux Tapestry' if you like. Now, imagine this representative wall-hanging encompasses every important moment in your character's life – a cradle-to-grave journey. If you took a frame to this canvas, placing it over the most significant period in your character's life, which moment would you focus on?

In effect, this is what you are doing with a play. Think of the stage as a microscope, focused on a specific group of characters at a specific time.

Don't bite off more than you can chew. I'm serious. Your audience will only have a couple of hours to spend in the company of these characters – so make sure that every moment counts.

Even the most straightforward characters will have hidden layers. If they don't, do they have any business being in your play in the first place? Probably not. For example, here's a scenario …

Todd and Rachel have been married for three years. They live a blissful and blameless existence in their cottage beside the sea, surrounded by their adoring (and adorable) friends and family.

OK, so where's the drama? Actually, as I was typing the above I found it impossible to suppress the little voice in my head as it screamed out 'the cottage is suffering from subsidence, and is slowly slipping into the sea'. Take that, Todd and Rachel – not so smug now, are you? And that's the irresistible instinct – to take things and shake them up to see what happens. And every time our characters recover from one obstacle we want to shove something else in their path. Oh, and Rachel's sleeping with the estate agent who sold them the damn cottage in the first place ...

Character tics

We all have little character tics that visually help to define us. I'm one of life's blinkers – especially if I'm tired or over-worked. I also realized recently how frequently I remove and wipe my glasses. It's become an extension of my personality – it's just one of the things I do. If I stopped to analyse this 'move' I'd say it was something I do to lend an air of gravitas. Basically, it's an attempt to prove I'm a fully formed 'grown up'. 'Look at me,' the movement seems to say. 'I'm an adult. See how carefully and thoroughly I wipe the lenses of my glasses.'

In life we often rely on 'props' – something to shift focus and distract attention. We don't want to be scrutinized too closely. Have you ever found yourself draining an already empty glass, just so you have something to do to help fill an uncomfortable silence? I do it all the time. This can communicate much about your character without needing any dialogue.

Set and props

Many literary managers and directors would argue that it's not the writer's job to think about set and props. People will often tell you not to worry about how your play will be realized on stage. A wise playwright, with foresight, will ignore this advice. Props don't magically materialize on stage. Remember, if a stuffed albatross appears in scene two, only to vanish again by the beginning of scene three – somebody will have to move it, dressed all in black, scampering around the set and pretending to be invisible.

In days gone by, audiences were fairly content to put up with scene changes that ran into several minutes. These days, I think our patience is running out.

I once had a character in a tin bath, and agonized about how a bath full of water could possibly be removed from the stage without sloshing all over the place. Believe me, it's not easy. In the end I placed the scene at the end of the act, so that the bath could be removed and the water emptied during the interval. And then the scene was cut anyway ...

Food

There's the wonderful old story of an actor who took the part 'because of a practical cake in act two'. I love food on stage. I love the rituals of eating, partly because they're *familiar* rituals. There can be something wonderful about enacting the commonplace on stage. The moment the aroma of cooking food spills out into the audience something magical happens. The preparation of food and the communal act of eating together can take on near-mystical properties. It's another way of drawing the audience into the world of your play – forging a deeper link between character and observer.

But do give a thought to budgetary considerations. I remember a director telling me once that the cost of supplying a fish every night nearly bankrupted the production of one of his plays.

'In vino, veritas'

'In wine, truth'. Alcohol loosens the tongue; it can cause your characters to drop their guard, to say too much, to reveal secrets. The consumption of alcohol and the knock-on effect on your characters can be a useful tool to help mark the passage of time. Alcohol can also give your characters a much needed shot of Dutch courage.

It could be seen as a bit of a cheat: an artificial and external means to unlocking information and revealing a character's innermost thoughts. However, as in life, alcohol in drama can become a useful social lubricant. It can draw characters together who may normally be polarly opposite. We've all been there, a couple of gin and tonics and it's a very short step to:

Me *(slurred)*. I love you, you're my best friend.

Where do I start my play?

'Writing the first draft means writing it wrong ...'

John McPhee

Are you a linear person? You see, I'm not. The thought of having to do *anything* chronologically terrifies me to my very marrow. Writing a play can be likened to an ascent of Everest and it's not made any easier when certain playwriting books have us believe that there's only one way of doing things. This is not one of those books. You have to find the way that's best for you. The ends justify the means.

It can be a really liberating experience to write out of sequence. You're taking ownership of the script. If you're finding it difficult to work on the first scene, why not try starting with scene three? Writing in this way I sometimes find the completed script creeps up on me by stealth, and that can be an eminently satisfying feeling.

Should I make a plan for my play, and then start writing? Or should I just start writing and see what happens?

Again, and I can't reiterate this enough, there's no set approach to writing a play. It all comes down to words on a page, and how you choose to put those words on the page is entirely up to you. If you're anything like me, the answer is simple. Start your play anywhere but the beginning.

> 'Eeyore was saying to himself, "This writing business. Pencils and what-not. Over-rated, if you ask me. Silly stuff. Nothing in it."'
>
> *A. A. Milne*

I can sometimes be slightly Eeyore-ish in my thinking. It's easy to believe that writing is always easier for other people, who probably dash off plays left, right and centre. When writing is going well, life is wonderful. When writing is going badly, your soul (or what you have left of it, dried-up husk of humanity that you are by this point) is in perpetual torment.

Working on your own, shut away in your office, can amplify the fears and paranoia that seem to particularly afflict writers. Resist the urge to scrap your play when the going gets tough – as it inevitably will at some point. If playwriting was the easiest job in the world, everybody would be doing it. Be under no illusions, it's difficult to write a play. And that's partly what makes it so rewarding when you finally complete a script.

Establishing a routine

I think playwrights tend to fall into one of two categories. First, the minority group – those writers who are so scrupulous in the way they order their working days that they never miss a deadline. Second, the majority group – those writers who lead a ramshackle existence and are consistent only in the sense that they have missed every deadline they've ever agreed to.

Two of the greatest resources at your disposal are time and patience. Allow yourself time to write, but be realistic. If you can't get it right, get it written. *Then* get it right. It takes the curse off it somehow.

How long will it take me to write a play? How many words should I write each day?

Imagine that you write for an hour a day and you can write 200 words in that hour. In ten days, writing 200 words a day you would have 2,000 words. In 100 days that's 20,000 words – or the equivalent of a full-length play. It's incredible how quickly a draft can begin to come together if you put your mind to it.

I think that's worth repeating, just so it sinks in:

200 words in an hour
2,000 words in 10 days
20,000 words in 100 days

(See how quickly it all adds up?)

My working day

7.00	The day begins. After a fifteen-minute jog and a breakfast of dry toast (1 slice) and half a grapefruit I feel a surge of creative energy.
7.30	I'm always at my desk by 7.30. Any later and I can feel my creative juices evaporating.
11.00	A quick cup of peppermint tea with ginseng (antioxidants keep my mind clear and alert).
11.00–18.00	SOLID WRITING TIME.
18.00–22.30	'Me' time.
22.30	And so to bed.

Shut the door of your work space and make yourself unavailable. If possible, try to keep regular office hours. If nothing else, it can have a normalizing effect to convince you that playwriting is actually a job of work. I'll be honest, as I write this I'm thinking 'what a bloody hypocrite'. Do I make myself unavailable? No. Do I keep regular office hours? Never.

So here's my *actual* workday:

My working day (version II)

7.00 The day begins – for some. I put my alarm on snooze and go back to sleep.

8.00   Get up, have breakfast.

10.30   Start writing.

13.45   Stop for lunch. Switch on the TV.

15.00   Wake up from delicious nap.

16.00–**Midnight**. Work fitfully, then finally pack it in for the day.

There's a lot to be said for calling it a day when you feel you could comfortably carry on writing. I think every writer reaches a pain threshold where every word committed to the page is painful. And the more painful it becomes, the less likely you are to spring out of bed in the morning, bright and fresh and raring to carry on where you left off.

Confessions

This is the way I work. Unconventional perhaps, but it's the only way that seems to make sense for me. I never write in order. I always build up random sections of script, until I feel I've got a large enough chunk of the play to print out. Then, I will take the script from my office into the lounge, and I'll sit on the floor and cut out each fragment of script, laying each piece carefully on the carpet. Next, I'll move these fragments around until I've worked out a suitable order and, with my trusty roll of Sellotape, I'll stick all these pieces together. When I've ended up with something resembling a long pianola roll, I'll go back into my office and start moving the text around on the screen. A more conventional, twenty-first-century form of cutting and pasting.

Of course, I'm left with a number of gaps where I lack the bridging section between two chunks of dialogue. I always write the word 'GAP' to clearly indicate this hole.

Next, I'll find a bridging line to join together each chunk of dialogue, removing each gap as I go. Sometimes this bridging line seems to come from nowhere and plainly doesn't work. The next process is slowly (sometimes unimaginably slowly) smoothing over these creaky sections of dialogue and gradually pulling the play together. It's rather like constructing a patchwork quilt (I imagine) – sewing together all the disparate sections so no holes remain. I would never encourage a writer to construct a play in this way, but it's the method that seems to work for me. I think I'd find it impossible to write a play any other way now.

The number of times I've seen people roll their eyes in despair or incredulity as I've attempted to explain my own specific way of working. I did work with a director once who was foolhardy enough to encourage me to work in a different way, and one that she found acceptable. Needless to say, we've never worked together since.

Some playwrights will ponder an idea for months before writing a single word; other writers would prefer to explore the play as they go along. Neither way is right, or the 'correct' way of working – it all depends on the individual writer. It boils down to one simple truth. As long as your process (no matter how ramshackle or eccentric) eventually leads to a production of the play, then that is the correct way for you to work. Don't question it, or feel you have to conform. After all, it's often the non-conformists who want to become playwrights in the first place.

What does a writer have on his/her desk?

You're going to spend a lot of time at your desk, so make sure you're comfortable – a workspace you can call your own. You need very little specialist equipment, you need very little space.

If you're anything like me, then you attract clutter like a magnet. A disorganized workspace can be symptomatic of a cluttered mind, but I refuse to be puritanical about my desk. I always have a mass of pens and pencils and attendant paraphernalia to hand. There's a photograph of my other half and bits and bobs to fiddle with – a clockwork gorilla, a china hippo, a magnifying glass. There's almost always a mug of tea and a biscuit if writing's going well (two biscuits if it's going badly).

To the left of my computer is a large granite pebble, engraved in copperplate writing with the words 'Nothing is written in stone'. When I'm staring hopelessly at the computer screen and everything I write seems wrong, I try to remind myself of that particular adage.

> 'It is better to have written a damned play, than no play at
> all – it snatches a man from obscurity.'
>
> *Frederic Reynolds*

You gaze out of a window, in a house on the intersection of two streets. Along one street you see a woman with a push-chair, on the other street you see a young man with an umbrella. You know that these people will meet before they know it themselves. This, I think, is what it feels like to be a playwright.

Now, to work ...

Some people like to write in complete silence, some people like to work with music on in the background. As with most aspects of writing, the rule of thumb is 'do what's best for you'.

Chances are you're a bit of a perfectionist. A lot of writers are. This is no bad thing. But don't beat yourself up unnec-essarily – it'll often get in the way of writing. Give yourself the permission to be terrible. Give yourself permission to get things wrong. Give yourself permission to write clunky sections of dialogue – knowing that you can return to them later and put them right. It's often the mistakes we make when writing that throw up the most exciting possibilities. Sometimes wrong can be halfway towards right.

Having a crack at things is good. The stakes are never as high as you think. Where will your idea take you? Even the most seasoned playwrights will still find they're surprised by the direction in which the play is taking them. And this is one of the pure joys of writing. You can find characters leading the play in directions you could not have predicted. A character will begin to assert his or her authority in the play. But if you're not happy …

There's nothing written that can't be undone

After all, there is a delete button! There's no way of shaping what you *haven't* written, so keep on typing and don't look back. It's better to have an entire play that needs work than one perfect scene. If that's too difficult, set yourself targets. 'I'll write ten pages, *then* I'll look back over what I've written.'

What do they mean by 'arrive late, leave early'?

Imagine you're going to a party. You don't want to arrive at seven when the host is laying out the nibbles, and the first few guests have arrived, engaged in agonizing small talk. Nor do you want to hang around after the life-and-soul types have gone home, and you're left with the stragglers. Imagine how boring that could be.

It's the same with a play. Don't provide unnecessary set-up or padding – get to the heart of the matter as swiftly as possible. It's often helpful to imagine that the mechanics of the play are already in motion before the curtain goes up. Your characters haven't suddenly sprung into existence, so what happened a week before the action of your play begins? A day before? An hour before? What happened in the minute before the lights came up on stage? If you stop to consider this, you may well find you're wasting less time with 'set-up' at the beginning of your play.

Think how the opening of your play may be changed by beginning with a question rather than a statement. You're looking to actively engage your audience.

The habit of writing

I remember reading once that it takes fourteen days for a habit to form. I'd happily go along with that. Writing quickly becomes a habit; the more you write, the more you want to write. And obviously, the more you want to write, the more likely you are to finish your play!

But if you're struggling to maintain a routine, take your pad or laptop and go and work somewhere else – a change is often as good as a rest. Remember, if it takes a long time or a short time to write a play, it's not necessarily a reflection on the quality of the work.

My mother often used to say 'Procrastination is the thief of time.' And she was right. But sometimes it is useful to break up the monotony of sitting in front of your computer screen. Do allow yourself regular tea breaks and a time for idle doodling.

So here is a page for doodles!

I'm a firm believer in active and passive writing. In that respect, writing is a peculiar occupation. You don't need to be slaving over your computer for things to begin falling into place. Whenever I'm struggling with a script I like to have a nice long walk to work things through in my head before returning to my desk. Sometimes it can be incredibly unproductive to thrash away at the computer in the hope that eventually things will come right.

But tell somebody that you're allowing an idea to slot into place inside your head and you can expect a certain amount of eye rolling and barely suppressed laughter. But it's perfectly true – we're writing all the time. Putting pen to paper (or finger to keyboard) is often only possible when we've got the idea straight in our heads.

Explaining the process of writing to a non-writer is akin to reeling off symptoms of mental imbalance. There are few jobs like this, and that's probably a good thing.

Don't forget to take a notebook with you when you're out and about, to scribble down any thoughts or snatches of conversation. If you haven't got room for a notebook, take a folded-up sheet of paper. Never be without pen and paper!

There is no reason on earth why writing a play can't be an enjoyable experience

Here's the truth (and whisper it softly), playwriting can actually be fun. Yes, really. This is an important point and well worth repeating:

There is no reason on earth why writing a play can't be an enjoyable experience.

There, now repeat that as a mantra. There's a simple four-letter word that people ignore at their peril. The word is 'play'. It's incredibly easy to find that you're getting so tied up with the theory of writing your play that you completely overlook the most important step in the process. You forget to … *write something!*

Be secretive. I can't reiterate this enough. Sharing too much information can have an unfortunately cathartic effect on your writing. The more you tell people about the play you're writing, the less reason you have to write it. So only give out information on a 'need to know' basis.

Nothing new under the sun

'Gozzi maintained that there can be but thirty-six dramatic situations. Schiller took great pains to find more, but he was unable to find even so many as Gozzi.'

Goethe

There are only so many possible dramatic configurations. Or, as my mother used to say, there is nothing new under the sun. Sometimes, in order to inject their work with as much originality as possible, writers are apt to rely on strange twists of fate and bizarre coincidences drawn from life. But here's the odd thing; often, when placed under the microscopic lens of the theatre, real-life incidents have a strange way of seeming false and unconvincing. I can't tell you the number of times I've heard writers say: 'Yes, I know it seems strange, but this did actually happen to me.'

Of course I've written about my own experiences, but I've dressed them up. Even people who've known me intimately for years might find it difficult to pinpoint moments in my work that are autobiographical. And to be honest, that's the way I think it should be. A transmogrification has to take place, converting your own life experiences into the lives of your fictional creations. The job of playwriting is about distilling thoughts and experiences and transposing them on the stage, making any necessary adjustments to protect ourselves, and codify that which is most personal to us.

'But it happened in real life, honest' is no argument for a dramatic set-up that fails to convince. There are only so many coincidences a play can sustain before an audience begins to question the believability of the world you're creating.

'Original' doesn't always translate as 'good'

Or, to put it another way, 'you *don't* gotta have a gimmick'. Be wary of originality for originality's sake. Don't misunderstand me, I'm all for innovation. But actually 'interesting' isn't always interesting. 'Boring' can be riveting.

What is my motivation?

'What is my motivation?' has become a bit of a theatrical cliché. But this is a vital question, except that a playwright will be approaching it from a slightly different angle. It's your responsibility to question the motivation of every single character in your play. Why are they behaving as they do? What are their objectives?

Go through the play scene by scene and chart the drama that drives the play forward, focusing on each individual strand of the story. What is it that's driving your play forward? Or, to put that another way, what is it that's holding your play back?

There are some people who think that writing a play gives you licence to bore an audience. It never does. If a scene or a section of dialogue is not driving the story forward, what's it doing there? Remind yourself what story you're trying to tell. Strip the play down to its most basic formula ...

'This is a play about....'

... something you can scribble down on a Post-it note and keep close to you at all times.

Courage, *mon brave*

It's always terrifying to sail off into uncharted waters, but the fear is also part of the fun – trust me!

No matter how well you plan the structure of your play, it's difficult to predict exactly what direction the writing will take you in once dialogue starts tumbling out on to the page and your characters begin to assert themselves. Your play is unexplored territory and you are writing the road map. You are the cartographer of your own play. With that knowledge comes a tremendous responsibility. As you make your way across this vast plain of unexplored dramatic terrain, you become aware of the myriad trails you can follow. And nothing can be more crippling than a limitless range of possibilities.

In a sense, every writer's journey is the same. It's about putting words on the page. Without words you obviously don't have a play. If this is your first play, the prospect of getting to the stage where your script is 'finished' and ready to send off can seem daunting. Don't expect to get everything right. How can you?

Think of your Post-it note as the skeleton of your play

So, imagine the formula you scribbled on your Post-it note, 'This is a play about ...', forms the basic structure of your play. You then add the muscle (the tensions and conflicts of each constituent scene in the play). Think of the dialogue as the skin that then holds everything together. What we don't want to see are the muscles and bones showing through the surface.

To a greater or lesser extent each and every scene is an intricate system of plants and pay-offs, like the ratchets and cogs in some mechanical apparatus.

The trick comes in disguising these mechanical processes. Make no bones about it, you're setting out deliberately to manipulate your audience. You are creating fictional characters, and placing them together in such configurations that your audience will laugh, cry, become incensed, terrified ...

Stage directions

Stage directions are always given from the actor's point of view. So stage left is the right-hand side of the stage to a member of the audience, and stage right is the audience member's left side of the stage. Get it?

There are many playwrights (and directors who agree with them) who feel their job is to suggest the world, but not explain how to conjure it up on stage. And then there are the megalomaniacs who want the world they have imagined to be recreated on stage with near-photographic accuracy.

It's obviously frustrating for a director to pick up a script and feel that the writer has gone out of his way to suggest how the play should be directed. The more unnecessary stage directions you write, the easier it is for a director to ignore everything you've written.

Do read through your play for stage directions. I once went through a script and stripped out about two thousand words of unnecessary description. The problem comes when a writer attempts to supplant the director by making all the decisions. It's not *your* job to direct the play. Nowadays, most writers tend to take up as little room as they can with stage directions, opting to dive into the dialogue as quickly as possible.

I used to get really carried away with stage directions, until a kindly literary manager helped me to see the light. Now I'm a reformed character. You're not writing a novel. Your narrative descriptions can be as elegant as you want, but they'll ultimately count for nothing. And if a director disregards all of your stage directions there's a real danger that anything of true significance may be lost as well. Far from helping, overly fussy stage directions can actually undermine the sense of your writing. They mark you out as a control freak, anxious to get your fingers in as many pies as possible. And if the director did heed every note, imagine how mechanical the performance would become. The rule of thumb is this: if a direction is vital to an understanding of the character or scene, leave it in. If it isn't, leave it out.

Here's an example of an unnecessary stage direction:

Jack (*cheerfully*): Happy birthday, Rachel.

Which begs the question, why *wouldn't* Jack cheerfully be wishing Rachel a happy birthday? So probably you'd want to get rid of 'cheerfully' – it's unnecessary here. Instead, we'd opt for:

Jack: Happy birthday, Rachel.

Now, suppose the line is intended to be delivered in a way that seems at odds with the sentiment. Maybe Jack has recently been dumped by Rachel?

Jack (*sarcastically*): Happy birthday, Rachel.

In that particular case you've probably earned the right to clarify the line.

Of course, there are those writers who go to the other end of the spectrum and provide no clues at all. I'll be honest, that breed of writer terrifies me. I'd never have the courage to cut back to such an extent. But then, as they say, horses for courses.

Should I just leave stage directions to the director, then? Aren't I allowed to say what I see in my head?

It's disconcerting for a director and actors to feel that a playwright is dogging their every move. But there are many directions that can be truly illuminating and well worth including. Think about how characters communicate in non-verbal ways. If a picture can say a thousand words, think what a shake of the head, a raised eyebrow or a smile can communicate:

She shrugs.

I love that sort of note. It somehow helps to drag us into the world of the play. No longer is your script simply a collection of words on a page. We can see in our mind's eye what that shrug looks like. But don't overload your script with this sort of note. Allow the director and actors to pick up on clues.

However, you can add as many notes and stage directions as you want while you're assembling your play. At this point it can be useful to do so. Think of it as the scaffolding that will be removed once you've finished constructing your script.

With a novel you're creating the entire product; with a stage play you're creating a fraction of the product. Without a director, actor, set and costume designer and the myriad departments who work behind the scenes, your play is nothing more than a pile of papers on a desk.

A play script is little more than a blueprint for production.

Keeping your audience in the dark

Imagine you've arrived late to watch a film at the cinema. You settle down in your seat and try to make sense of the fifteen lost minutes. Does your brain explode under the crushing weight of bafflement? No. Little by little you piece together the clues. You work out that the hero is called Lionel; that he's been separated from his wife (Holly) for six years; that it was an alien attack on New York that has led to the zombie epidemic; and that in spite of all the above, Lionel has never stopped loving Holly.

There are impenetrable films that may be the exception to the rule here – but chances are you wouldn't have understood even if you'd made it for the opening credits.

Keep your audience in the dark for as long as possible. Believe me, they'll end up thanking you.

Picture the geography of your on-stage world

Suppose housemates Todd and Ben are planning to cheer up their friend Rachel by taking her out for a night on the town. Rachel has spent the day in her pyjamas watching TV:

> **Rachel:** I suppose I should go and get dressed.
> *She exits.*
> **Todd:** Where do you fancy going?
> **Ben:** Dunno. We could try that new Italian place.
> *Rachel returns, dressed for a night out.*
> **Rachel:** So what do you think?

Clearly, the time that has elapsed between Rachel's exit and return is not long enough for this metamorphic change. If Rachel has been anticipating the night out, and is already dressed beneath her robe, then fine. But that's not what's happening here.

Think about the three-dimensional world of your play. When your characters leave the stage, where exactly do they go? If Rachel leaves the sitting room and runs upstairs to her bedroom, that journey may well take her twenty seconds. Imagine she takes another five minutes to dress. Then another twenty seconds to run back downstairs and into the sitting room. If this scene is unfolding in 'real time', Todd and Ben would need enough dialogue to cover Rachel's absence. Think of the geography of your own house.

Be clear in your mind about the geography of the set – how one room relates to another. If the action of your play takes place in one room, work out the geography *around* that room. Presumably this room isn't stranded in time and space. If one of your characters exits through a door, where does it lead her? Into another room? If so, what room? Or does the door take the character outside the house? It's up to you.

Remember that your characters presumably exist before they appear on stage, and the energy they carry with them in this off-stage world they will then carry on stage. The energy of one character can impact positively or negatively on the energy of another character.

Create as much or as little back-story for your characters as you want. Some playwrights will want to know everything about their characters before they put pen to paper, other writers are content to adopt a more laidback approach. Again, don't feel there's only one way to do this, and don't allow yourself to be bullied into believing it's somehow a failing if you don't have all the answers as you set out to write your script. I think mapping out a play too narrowly can create a sense of pressure that can ultimately prove destructive. Allow yourself some wriggle room.

How can you know for certain what your characters' reactions will be to any given situation? You haven't had a chance to explore them yet. Allow yourself the freedom to stray from the path. As you write you will discover who your characters are. It's amazing how characters can begin to grow on the page – fighting for space and dominance in the play.

Do characters change while you are writing them?

For me, always. The process of writing the first draft is partly about the discovery of who your characters truly are, their tastes and predilections. Words have a way of popping into their mouths. But if the dialogue is interchangeable, obviously there's a problem. Think of the rhythm of speech. Put your hand over the character names. Can you work out which character is speaking? If you could easily switch character names, then it's worth going back through the dialogue to fine-tune.

Make sure each of your characters has their own distinctive 'voice'. Think again of those conversational tics we overhear all the time, which almost become punctuation marks to break up an exchange and add emphasis.

Are there any rules about swearing, etc.?

I'll be honest with you; I have absolutely no qualms about the use of 'bad language' in the theatre – as long as it earns its place. And that's the litmus test. It needs to come out of the mouths of the characters, not out of the mouth of the playwright. But is it necessary? Is it simply being added in to make the play seem edgy and contemporary – or to compensate for deficiencies in the script? Be under no illusions, a rat will always be sniffed out. Nothing will make a greater impact than a well-written play.

When I first started writing I was convinced the only way I was going to make it was by sitting down and churning out a play about violent crime or heroin addiction. Thankfully, in the end I didn't try. And that's the point really. Chances are if I had attempted to bash out that sort of script, it would have rung hollow. It wouldn't have been my own voice.

It's always dangerous trying to surf trends. As with any trend, if you can sense a rising tide you've probably missed the boat already. Don't forget that many theatres programme months, or years, in advance. Many projects take a long time to come to fruition. So write the play you want to write, rather than the play you feel current trends are dictating.

Some first-time writers spend so much time striving to be challenging and ground-breaking that they completely overlook one important aspect of playwriting. They forget to make their play any good.

The best way to get noticed is by writing a damn good play.

I am a middle-aged woman. Is there less chance of my work being accepted?

There's no doubt that the theatre has been a male-dominated profession. But things are changing. The cult of youth is certainly prevalent in the theatre. But look at the writers who continue to produce plays when they are well past retirement age. When I first started writing I was encouraged to remain a twenty-four-year-old for a couple of years. Unfortunately there comes a point where honesty and the ageing process catch up.

Actually, I'm not convinced that the theatre is really that age obsessed. I think it all depends on the play you're writing. Theatre is a very broad church. I can think of several venerated and venerable playwrights who continue to be successful well into their seventies. I recently read a review of a play written by a playwright in his nineties. It does happen.

And we're off …

A friend went to the theatre. Sitting in front of him was an elderly man: his wife on one side, his son on the other. Throughout the play the elderly man crackled a sweet wrapper between thumb and forefinger. The noise wasn't loud enough to halt the production, but it was loud enough to completely ruin the friend's enjoyment of the play. As the performance finished and the audience began to leave the theatre, the friend finally decided to confront the man and make a point of principle.

'Do you know what you were doing?' asked the friend.

'No,' replied the man.

'You were crackling a sweet wrapper,' continued the friend. 'You completely ruined the play for me.'

Later that evening the friend happened to discover the name of the elderly sweet-wrapper rustler. The name sounded familiar. The friend went home and Googled the name. It turned out that the sweet-rustler was a well-known Holocaust survivor.

The drama here isn't in the situation (although fascinating in a cringe-making way), but in the character's *reaction* to the situation. Because it's the reaction that helps us to define the character. Of course, the friend in question was mortified when he made this discovery. But what if he was so self-absorbed he still thought, 'Hell, I made a valid point. He *was* ruining the performance for me.' Do we have sympathy for this 'character'? Where could we take this?

You don't have to sit in judgement of your characters. It's not your job to draw conclusions about their actions and behaviour. I think it's extremely difficult to raise the enthusiasm to write a character who is truly 'good' (and I can't think of a single actor who would thank you if you did).

Conversely, I think it's nigh on impossible not to have a little bit of love for a character who is regarded as thoroughly despicable by all the other characters in the play. There's a perverse satisfaction to be had in treating your characters in this way. I think if you love or despise your characters in the writing, there's a very real danger that they will end up on the page as two-dimensional cutouts.

How much detail do I need to give about characters' ages, physical appearance, costume, etc.?

Sometimes it is helpful to be specific about a character's age, especially if explicit reference is made in the script. For example, a character reaches their sixteenth birthday in the course of the play, or the play leaps in time so we see a character at the ages of twenty-four and forty-four.

Be careful not to over-egg the pudding. I often think back to those great plays of the early twentieth century, where a playwright fills the whole of the first page with a minutely detailed description of the set and principal characters. Something along these lines ...

> *A tumbledown tenement building on the outskirts of Dublin. Flather enters, a man of fifty-seven, sinewy, with thinning auburn hair, greying at the temples. His face is pockmarked, his eyes are hollow. He whistles the opening bars of 'When Irish Eyes are Smiling' ...*

Now where would you even begin to track down such an actor? In the pages of the Spotlight casting directory, or down a deep, dark pit? Overstuff your script with this sort of obsessive detail and you won't be admired for your prescriptive vision. Chances are you'll be marked out as a troublemaker!

Best to be brief and to the point:

Sharon, early twenties.

Or

Mal, late sixties.

Give any relevant information as swiftly as possible and then move on.

Is it true you need to say something more than once for an audience to remember it? How can I prevent exposition from becoming boring?

Some writers dispense with exposition altogether. The play is left as a riddle for the audience to decipher (or not). On the other hand, it is worth bearing in mind that an audience doesn't have a chance to pause the play and re-wind. It's not like a novel. If we get confused and lose our place, we can't just turn back a chapter for a brief re-cap. Even the most intelligent audience members can find their attention wandering, and not always because of deficiencies in the play. They may be fumbling in a bag, checking to make sure they've switched off their mobile phone at precisely the same time as a vital piece of storyline is unfolding on stage.

... HOWEVER ...

Don't ever try to spoon-feed your audience. Take this exchange, for example:

Max: Hi, Mary. How are you?
Mary: You know. OK. You know Jay and me are getting a
    divorce?

Max: Yeah. Sam told me.

Mary: How is Sam?

Max: OK.

Mary: I haven't seen her since the accident.

Max: Yeah. That's the last time I'm letting her climb up a
twenty-foot ladder.

Just the sort of thing we want to avoid. OK, so imagine we
have two new characters, let's call them Dan and Amy. They
meet in a coffee shop:

Dan: Hi, Amy. How are you?

Amy: Fine, Dan. Fine.

This is plausible exposition, obviously, but we're left with
the feeling that the names 'Dan' and 'Amy' have been
dropped into the exchange entirely for the benefit of the
audience. Let's try it a different way and insert a third character, Jess:

Jess: Dan … you've met Amy?

Dan: Yes. Hi.

Amy: Hi.

It's still exposition, but we've swept it under the carpet. A
little more surreptitious. Exposition is sometimes logical. It
can also be appropriate for specific characters. For example,
we could perhaps forgive a more expositional form of dialogue in an older character, but I'm not convinced that we're
so forgiving when it comes to a younger character.

But generally speaking, the more information you
provide for your audience, the less reason they have to
think for themselves.

Landlines versus the mobile phone

The dawn of telephonic communication brought with it many opportunities for the canny dramatist. It offered the perfect way to smuggle in vital information – exposition, but dressed up:

> **Rachel:** He did what … with the doctor's receptionist … for how long? Three months. But he's only been married four months.

The telephone almost became a character in its own right, and with a ringing bell could announce itself with a sense of pomp and ceremony that is sadly lacking in modern mobile communication.

And when it suited a dramatist for this newly harnessed technology to malfunction, it was the work of a moment to achieve just that. Telephone lines could be blown down in a storm, or severed deliberately. In the good old days, Agatha Christie could write a play with half a dozen characters shut away in an isolated manor house, with a crazed murderer happily picking off his or her victims one by one, safe in the knowledge that the nearest constabulary was five miles away by bicycle and the telephone was conveniently out of action.

But the mobile phone has robbed the world of this suspense. Nowadays, when trapped in similar circumstances, at least one character would be able to find a signal and dial for help.

Contemporary plays will perhaps age more quickly than was once the case as we attempt to get a handle on modern technology and keep our plays bang up to date. Depending on your views on mobile technology, people are perhaps worse today at communicating than they were just a decade or so ago. It's rare to get through a ten-minute chat with my brother or sister without a couple of text messages being received or sent, effectively creating a hiatus in the conversation. We live in a world where information is rapidly disseminated – on TV, through the internet, on mobile phones. Just think how a web search has impacted on stories of mistaken identity – 'You thought this was Professor Amstrong? Surely you Googled him first?' Nowadays we can verify a character's identity at the touch of a button.

Alas, for a playwright, the dawn of this digital age has made it more difficult to hide, assume a false identity, or pull the wool over someone's eyes.

Should I write dialect or let the actor find it?

Do try to cultivate an ear for accents. A specific regional dialect can add a rich dimension to the dialogue. It is helpful not to constrict actors too much with dialect, as lines can sometimes become almost impossible for an actor to deliver. If you need the Rosetta Stone to decode a line, that could be problematic.

Truth and Lies

'The subject of drama is The Lie. At the end of the drama THE TRUTH – which has been overlooked, disregarded, scorned, and denied – prevails. And that is how we know the Drama is done.'

David Mamet

My tastes can be surprisingly low rent. I love detective dramas, I can easily find myself hooked on soaps. Soap operas are all about the 'hook'. It's what keeps us watching from one episode to the next. But more than that, it's what keeps us watching from one *scene* to the next.

I was watching a soap on TV the other day. I counted over forty lies in a single episode. It's the same with a detective drama. Unless we see the clues, we won't get the chance to play along and attempt to work out 'who done it'.

In my youth (when I should have been writing) I would often telephone a friend to compare notes on the outrageous clothes that characters had been wearing in re-runs of *Ironside*. I knew I had a problem. But I like to think my misspent youth has practical applications. Think of any good detective drama. Our attention is deliberately drawn to the clues, the motives, the alibis. Even apparently trivial detail will feed into the plot. Oscar Wilde said some good things about triviality and I've always taken heart from that. Everything signifies. And if it didn't, it wouldn't be there.

Lies are often the fuel that keeps the engine of the drama ticking over. Just think of the 'soap opera clinch' when two lovers are reconciled in an embrace, but over the boyfriend's shoulder we see the veil of doubt in the girlfriend's eyes. Dum-dum-dum!

Lies are the stock-in-trade of a good soap opera. Rarely does a character make it through an episode without fibbing.

The conflict comes when the lie is found out – as it invariably is. If it wasn't, there wouldn't be any conflict. Without conflict there's no drama. And without drama ... there's no play.

A tell-tale trait of many plays by first-time playwrights is the disconcerting habit the characters have of telling the truth all the time. Again, don't feel you have to make your characters *likeable*. Think of the yin and the yang. In every bad person there's some good, in every good person there's a little bad. If characters lack that balance, an audience quickly loses interest.

Empowering an audience

So imagine you've got two friends in a long-term relationship. Michelle tells you how in love she is, and she's sure her relationship with Matt is really going places. She's already planning the wedding, and thumbing through books of baby names. The trouble is, you've had a conversation with Matt the day before and he's desperately trying to find the right moment to break up with Michelle. Imagine an audience watching this scene play out. If you've also shown the audience the previous scene, think how that alters things. It really helps to ratchet up the tension. You have empowered them with additional information so that they are a step ahead and fully appreciate the sense of mounting tension and can anticipate the eventual inevitable showdown between Michelle and Matt.

Births, deaths and marriages

Think of all those special occasions and family gatherings that a playwright gleefully falls upon. They're the dramatist's equivalent of the wooden horse, using a 'special occasion' as a legitimate pretext for smuggling in an eclectic band of characters that are positively guaranteed to rub each other up the wrong way. A family event often comes along to screw up the relative calm of everyday life. Birthdays, weddings, funerals – for a playwright, these potentially awkward social occasions are heaven sent. In most cases, we can avoid conflict and confrontation to a certain extent. We simply absent ourselves. But it's not always possible. There are certain situations we find difficult to avoid.

How long should a scene be?

This is one of those 'how long is a piece of string?' questions. As a rule of thumb, try not to outstay your welcome. Make your point and move on. Be strict with yourself. Think about pace – the internal speed and rhythm of your play. Vary the length of each scene. Never allow your play to fall into a predictable rhythm.

If the length of each scene is so regular you could run your watch by it, stop and think.

How many scenes does a play need?

In recent years there's been a tendency for plays to get shorter and shorter. I think it's true to say that our television viewing habits have had some impact on this. We're used to TV dramas lasting fifty minutes to an hour, and I think a lot of people's attention spans begin to wander after this.

Unlike TV or radio, your play won't be expected to come in at a specific length. If it runs for two hours, fine, if it's longer, again nobody's going to be standing over you with a stopwatch. If it's shorter, that's not a problem. If an audience is fully engaged with a play it shouldn't matter how long the script is. It *shouldn't* – but at the same time it *does*. Does the act earn its length? It doesn't take long to get a sense of a play dragging and an audience growing restless.

As a rough guide, a double-line-spaced play will probably read at a minute or a minute and a half per page.

Intervals

An interval can be a useful opportunity for marking a geographical shift or a leap in time. It's also useful for a substantial change of set.

There are certainly benefits to not having an interval. It's easier to immerse the audience in the world of the play, without breaking the spell by interrupting the action.

You can create an additional dramatic intensity if the play runs straight through without a break in proceedings. Depriving an audience of the opportunity to discuss the play in the interval can work to your advantage. But audiences can become restive and their minds wander, often settling on the following thoughts:

'I need the loo. I want an ice cream. I wonder if it's too late to buy a programme?'

Some theatres rely on interval bar turnover (and when you get your bill you can understand why). But the break in the action must serve a dramatic purpose as well. Many theatres would be loath to miss out on the extra revenue an interval can provide, but I'm happy to say that few artistic directors would put capitalist gain ahead of dramatic integrity. There's no reason the audience can't get oiled up after the performance.

Be careful not to wrap up your act so neatly that it seems like a conclusion in itself. You want to leave your audience wanting more, not feeling like they've reached the end of something.

Think about *what* an audience takes away with them during the interval. Most audience members don't stop engaging with the play the moment the house lights come up. They don't stay trapped in some sort of theatrical stasis for the duration of the interval – say, twenty minutes or so. In between forcing their way to the bar, or negotiating the queue for the toilets, the play continues to occupy their minds, and consequently their conversations. If the play has ended on a cliffhanger, it's only natural to attempt to second-guess the resolution. We have problem-solving minds; we don't observe the action passively.

In the past there was often no clearly thought-through dramatic logic to the break after act one. It just happened to fall halfway through proceedings. The second act would pick up where the first act left off, with the characters standing in exactly the same positions they held as the curtains came down. But a second act can be a far more exciting prospect than this. It can be a chance to break all the rules you so painstakingly set up in the first act of your play. You can even go off in a completely different direction altogether.

On press night you might be grateful for an interval. I always am (I'm the one in the cold sweat with a glass of whisky to steady my nerves).

Where do I start act two?

Remember, as an audience take their seats for the second act of your play, you want to challenge them as you reel them back into your world …

It's easy to get to the point where you're overwhelmed by choices and possible dramatic permutations, especially in the second act. Don't opt for the easy route and follow the path of least resistance. What you're looking for is the path of most resistance.

It's a bit like a runaway train. Throughout the play you've

been travelling inexorably to the top of a hill. As your play reaches its conclusion the brakes fail, taking with it your characters as it plunges down into the ravine and eventually reaches the end of the line. The play gathers momentum as the characters' objectives drive them through to the climax and resolution of your play. It's this drive and momentum we're looking for. You need a heart-quickening moment of dramatic climax.

For the audience, the 'problem solving' process continues. By now they have almost certainly begun to pre-empt the conclusion of your play. You've provided them with the clues, and like detectives they're piecing things together. There can be few things as unsatisfactory as predicting an end of a play only to be proved correct. Keep the audience on their toes.

Be careful not to end the play too tidily – it can seem forced and unconvincing. Think of those Victorian and Edwardian plays where a letter arrives on a silver salver, informing all and sundry that things are not quite as they seemed …

Lady Marksby: You mean –?
Dr Fitzgerald casts his eye over the letter.
Dr Fitzgerald: I mean, Lady Marksby, that Gerald is undoubtedly your son after all.
Lady Marksby: Gerald, I was wrong to doubt you. Can you ever find it in your heart to forgive me?
Gerald: Of course Mother.
Dr Fitzgerald: But what of Myrtle, the between-stairs maid?
Lady Marksby: Relations between you and my son must end forthwith. I'm sorry, my child.
Myrtle: Begging your pardon, Ma'am.

Gerald: She's not really Myrtle, Mother.

Myrtle: I must apologize for the subterfuge, Lady Marksby. My real name is Millicent, youngest daughter of the Second Viscount Braeburn. I was in disguise, to make quite certain of Gerald's true feelings for me before I revealed that I am to inherit a fortune when my dear father dies.

Gerald: And I was not found wanting, Mother. Millicent and I are in love.

Lady Marksby: Gerald. My dear boy.

Gerald and Lady Marksby embrace. Gerald embraces Myrtle.
   Dr Fitzgerald gazes upon the scene and smiles indulgently.
Curtain.

See what I mean? All rather too convenient.

How do I decide whether something should happen on stage or off stage?

Years ago I watched Steven Berkoff standing on stage, throwing an imaginary beach ball into the wings. He then caught the ball as though it had been returned to him. Not only did this imply the presence of a second character, but it gave the audience an opportunity to create that character in their minds.

Never underestimate the power of the off-stage world. A character that is referred to but never seen can become the most important character in the play, because they exist entirely in the imagination of the audience. However, if the off-stage world is more interesting and powerful than the on-stage world, it's certainly worth asking yourself whether your focus is wrong.

Violence on stage

Be careful about on-stage violence. Often the metaphorical 'violence' of well-constructed character conflict is more convincing and dramatically satisfying than a fist fight could ever be. Also, a 'real' fight can be difficult to stage authentically. A punch that's utterly convincing to one section of the audience may fail to convince if an audience member happens to be sitting elsewhere in the auditorium. Even the most experienced of fight co-ordinators can struggle to make a fight sequence entirely realistic on stage.

Writing comedy

> 'I am all for incest and tortured souls in moderation, but a good laugh from time to time never hurt anybody.'
>
> *P.G. Wodehouse*

Who said drama can't be funny? When somebody invites me to the theatre and adds, 'Oh, by the way, it's a comedy,' it's like manna from heaven. 'Laugh and the world laughs with you.' But never let anybody try to convince you that writing a comedy is somehow easier than penning a straight play.

Years ago I used to play a ridiculous game with a friend, which we called 'Obvious I Spy'. The aim of the game was to be as obvious as possible.

'I spy, with my little eye, something beginning with D ...' my friend would say, staring at a dog, dishwasher, or desk. Ridiculous, I know, but it passed the time.

I was trying to figure out the way to begin a play. I knew it would involve characters sitting round a coffin, and I wanted to give the audience an early opportunity to relax into the play and, ideally, laugh. It struck me that it might be possible to revive the game of 'Obvious I Spy …'

Act One

The front parlour of the Post Office, St Martin's. A coffin stands on trestles, down stage. Four chairs. Lights up. Tommy and Ben sit in silence. At a distance, dressed in excessively sombre clothing, sits the figure of Frank Gunwallow. Long pause.

> Tommy: I spy wi' my liddle eye, summin' beginnin' with …
> *Pause.*
> … C.
> *He stares hard at the coffin.*
> Ben: Coffin?
> *Pause.*
> Tommy: Well?
> Ben: Well what?
> Tommy: Your turn.
> Ben: Eh?
> Tommy: I spy wi' my liddle –

The sparseness of the set helped the moment enormously. It pointed up the ridiculousness of the situation.

If we're trying to forge a relationship as quickly as possible between a character and the audience, there's a lot to be said for getting a joke in early. It breaks down the audience's defences, acting like an ice-breaker in a room full of anxious dinner guests. In other words, the audience lower their guard.

I've always liked the term 'black comedy' – it seems to cover a multitude of sins. Actually, it's not all that difficult to make an audience laugh. But is that laugh the *right* laugh?

There's nothing worse than the writer's 'hand of god' appearing, steering the characters into amusing situations. Don't allow your characters to become subordinate to set-up and gags. Ideally the humour will always be character led.

The past is a foreign country. Or is it ...?

Deciding to set a play in the past can open up a whole host of dramatic possibilities. But be clear about why you have chosen to set your play in the past. As with any other play, work out *why* you want to tell this story. It needs to have a resonance for you and ultimately for your audience.

Why are you setting your play in the past? What does a historical drama convey that a contemporary drama could not? You want to write it because it's an interesting story. Sure, but it's not enough simply to be *interesting*. The play needs vitality, it needs to speak powerfully of the human condition, regardless of the fact that the story may be set two, three, even four hundred years ago. What will this historical event communicate to a contemporary audience?

Becoming an expert

It's good to be an enthusiast. In the past couple of years I've had to get up to speed with museum design, Soviet politics of the mid-1930s and cake baking, all labours of love (particularly the cake baking).

Every play demands a certain amount of research, and it's surprising how willing many people will be if approached to help with your research. Often you're engaging with someone's specialist interest, and they'll be delighted to pass on some of this knowledge.

Don't allow research to get in the way of writing!

The research material, no matter how fascinating, needs to be given shape by the writer to instil a palpable sense of forward dramatic momentum. It's very easy to find that you've accumulated a mass of interesting research that's just getting in the way of writing the play. There's nothing more damaging than becoming a slave to the research material.

It can be painful to jettison the research that you've gathered so painstakingly. Best to think that it's enriching your script in a subtle way, because it almost certainly is.

Should you research first, or as you go along?

I know several playwrights who write their plays and then research retrospectively. There is an argument for writing your play this way round, getting the historical facts to fit the dramatic arc of your play. This may seem a disingenuous way of working, but never lose sight of the fact that you are writing a play.

What are the rules about using real-life people in a play?

You can't libel the dead. But don't think it's 'open season' on any deceased personality. Be careful. Be sensitive. If your intention is character assassination you can hardly blame any surviving family members if they're reluctant to help with your research.

When you set out to write a biographical play you almost

instantly enter the realms of speculation. Do you know for a *fact* that is what your character said? Well, of course not. Even a transcription of a known historical meeting will seem leaden if transposed from page to stage. Although idioms of speech may be true to the period they may seem wholly unconvincing to a contemporary audience.

Ideally, the subject should reach out to us from the past. If their story is set in aspic, unable to make a connection with a contemporary audience, then there's a problem. So be careful not to write a dry museum piece.

It's your job as playwright to cast light on your subject in a way that a biographer rarely can. You're reanimating dusty bones and perhaps bringing a long-dead figure to life in front of the audience's eyes.

Don't just rely on second-hand knowledge. The internet isn't always the most reliable fount of knowledge, so do check and double-check your sources.

Probe as deeply as you can to discover the 'truth' of your character. But beware – once you get a feel for your subject it can be a rather hypnotic and addictive process. If you're a bit of a 'completist' like me, it's tempting not to commit a word to the page until you feel you have a comprehensive knowledge of the subject matter. But give yourself a break.

There is also the danger of trying too hard to impress an audience with the depth and complexity of your research. Be sure to wear your knowledge lightly.

Beware the cradle-to-grave drama

A cradle-to-grave epic is all very well, but does it serve the story you want to tell? As with any play, be selective about your focus. You may want to cram in as much of your subject's life as possible because you find it deeply fascinating. But again, are you quite certain that it's *dramatic*? It's easy to find yourself distracted by the wealth of research material available. But remember, you're not an archivist. That's somebody else's job.

> 'The historian, essentially, wants more documents than he can really use; the dramatist only wants more liberties than he can really take.'
>
> *Henry James*

A little bit of good in everyone

Of course, as discussed before, there's no such thing as an entirely good person – or, conversely, an entirely bad person. We're all shades of the two – sometimes more one than the other. But there's a balance. Imagine a playwright sits down to write a play about Genghis Khan. The writer would have to find the kernel of humanity in the man, or the play would have no texture. It's always good to avoid writing uncomplicated saints and sinners, especially when dealing with 'real life' characters.

Where in time are we?

Imagine you're going to write a play about Charles Darwin. Do you choose to dramatize the moment that he hits upon the idea of sitting down to write *On the Origin of Species*? Or do you travel back in time, to show the young Darwin mulling things over? Or both? Time is an elastic commodity. Remember, you set up your own parameters here.

What you don't want is a rehashing of the same old story. Try to approach events from a slightly more oblique angle. Investigate lesser-known incidents in the lives of your characters. You might also choose to deliberately misinterpret the life of your character. But tread cautiously, because you tread on their dust.

If I'm writing a play about a specific subject, and I then hear a play is being produced dealing with the same subject, should I continue, or just scrap the play?

I have to say, this is particularly problematic if you start working on a biographical play. You can never tell for sure that you're the only writer researching this character.

I can't begin to tell you how frustrating it is to discover that another writer (usually a more successful one) has written a play that is eerily similar to the idea you're working on. Sometimes there may be fewer similarities than you initially imagine.

Once you've got over the initial shock, sit down and work out whether there really is an overlap of subject matter. Often it's not as bad as it seems.

Many's the time I've sat down to watch a documentary on TV and thought 'that would make a great idea for a play', only to ponder how many other playwrights are sitting in front of the TV thinking exactly the same thing. Of course, there are topics that are tackled time and time again – look how frequently it happens in the cinema. It doesn't necessarily mean you have to ditch the idea altogether. Sometimes there might be an entirely different route into the play. One door has closed, but miraculously another door has swung open.

I remember the pain of discovering that not one, but *two,*

plays were being written about a literary figure I'd been researching on and off for several years. It was stinging – an emotional kick to the guts. Strangely, though, as the weeks passed and the bitterness ebbed away, I realized that I'd actually been presented with a fantastic opportunity to reassess my initial idea. I thought, 'OK, so how can I approach the subject matter in a slightly more off-kilter way?' It was the little jolt I needed.

Perversely, it's sometimes the way that the more obscure the idea, the greater the risk you take.

Co-writing a play

Co-writing is not everybody's cup of tea. The act of writing can be an intensely personal thing, and there are many people who would feel exposed by having to let another writer in on this process. But for those writers who are pre-pared to make a leap of faith, there can be encouraging benefits.

Until recently, the thought of penning a play with another writer seemed odd and unsettling. Now it seems as natural as drawing air. I meet my writing chum at his office, and an assistant brings us cups of tea, chocolate biscuits and indi-vidual sherry trifles. Not only am I getting a lot written very quickly, I'm also putting on weight.

I think on occasions you're also more likely to take greater risks as you bat lines of dialogue backwards and forwards, although it perhaps helps if one of the writing partners takes the lead in typing up notes, otherwise it can quickly resemble a game of consequences. It might take a while to find your feet, and work out the most pragmatic and suc-cessful way of conducting this new writing partnership.

The obvious advantage is being able to walk into production meetings and rehearsals with your co-writer beside you for moral support.

Writing for a younger audience

Many playwrights lament the passing of the large-cast play. Writing for a young cast or community theatre project can sometimes help to redress the balance. Although a number of books have been published to guide authors through the process of writing fiction for a younger readership, it's extremely difficult trying to find an equivalent publication dealing with drama for a similar age range.

Writing for younger audiences can be an extremely liberating experience. For a long time there was a dearth of suitable material for both younger audiences and younger casts. Too often there was a desire to educate at the expense of entertaining.

Don't think for one minute that writing for young people is somehow easier than writing for an adult audience. It really isn't. The trouble is that many people (dramatists included) see youth theatre as an inferior dramatic form. It's also a mistake to assume that you're writing for a less sophisticated audience.

There are certain pragmatic considerations that should be taken into account when writing for a younger cast. In stark contrast to the advice that playwrights are normally given, writing for a large cast is positively encouraged. The important thing is to try to capture the voices of the characters you are writing for. This may seem an obvious point, but it is easy to succumb to the pitfall of writing your characters as 'little adults' rather than 'big children'.

There is a tendency to approach writing for a younger audience in the wrong way. To think 'OK, then, what *can't* I write?' The road to dramatic hell is paved with good intentions.

One of the biggest hurdles to overcome is the feeling that your play must be 'worthy'. Plays can suffer because of a writer's miscalculated *need* to educate the audience. Write the play you want to write, don't allow yourself to be drawn into the trap of writing the sort of play you *think* you should be writing for your target audience. Writers often fail to appreciate just how sophisticated their audience really is.

In most cases, if your play is written to be performed by young people it's worth remembering that there will be an uneven ratio between male and female performers. A greater weighting of female roles is often advisable, although don't discount the possibility of cross-casting.

Can characters swear?

The use of 'bad' language is always a contentious issue, and I touched on this subject earlier in the book. Of course, it all depends where the play is going to be performed. Theatre in Education (TIE) companies may well impose restrictions on the language used in commissioned plays. It's all very well to be ground-breaking and controversial, but if this results in the play being pulled from production, it will be a hollow victory.

If you're writing a play for a youth theatre company, especially one that's affiliated to a metropolitan or regional theatre, you may have greater flexibility. Here's an example, from my play *Multiplex*, which was commissioned by the National Theatre for their Connections programme – plays written specifically to be performed by young companies:

Spike: The thing about school, the teachers always seem to think if you're bright you want to learn. Like how wrong can you get? Can't wait to get out the fucking place. I can count to ten in three languages, so I reckon I'm educated enough. GCSE revision would be a fuck of a lot easier without the teachers there to distract me. Maths, English ... piece of piss. So I spend half my time trying to find ways to get thrown out. So many foolproof ways. Art, for instance, a gleaming example. You could shit on a piece of paper and call it postmodernist sculpture. So I did. This does not impress old Mr Vincent. 'Call this art?' he says, 'Yes, sir,' I said, 'very Tracey Emin, don't you think, sir?' 'Tracey Emin, my arse,' he says. 'It's a load of crap, that's what it is,' and we all piss ourselves laughing, 'cause that's exactly what it is. 'It just won't wash,' he says. 'This is state education, not the fucking Tate Modern.' He said buggering, not fucking, but I think fucking's what he meant. We call him The Dick, old Mr Vincent, 'cause he's a bit of a dick. The clue's in the nickname. And the tosser says, 'Spike, you always have to have the last word.' So I say, 'Yes.' So then I get suspended, which means I can have a lie-in. Don't need to get up. Dad's pissed off to bugger-knows-where with Gran's care assistant, and Mum's on the alcopops, so basically my life's my own. And our deputy head, he's a prick, he keeps phoning up and saying, 'You can come back to school as soon as you've learnt your lesson. Have you learnt your lesson yet?' So of course I say, 'Not yet, sir. Might take another week or two.' And the twat can't think of nothing to say, so he says goodbye and hangs up, and I go back to watching porn on cable. *Beat.*
Cushy number really, school.

84

Of course, a good play will also appeal to adult audience members. In most cases it will be adults buying the tickets, often accompanying their children to see the play, but don't forget that you're targeting the younger sections of the audience. There can be a danger that by attempting to appease the whole family, the play ultimately appeals to no one.

Degree courses

A growing number of universities offer playwriting as part of their degree courses. I was very lucky to have a very strong playwriting course at my own university, run by a charismatic lecturer from the States. He seemed slightly rattled that none of us admitted to writing under the influence of drugs or alcohol. We just weren't that rock and roll. Personally, I write under the influence of nothing more stimulating than a cup of tea and the occasional biscuit. As a wise man once said, 'Tea is the drug'.

As a former playwriting lecturer myself, I urge you to write what you want to write and resist the urge to over-intellectualize your writing. This is a creative exercise and not an academic one. Make the most of this opportunity. Don't feel your writing has to be crammed full of postmodernist theory. Believe me, if an audience might find this dry and unpalatable fodder, chances are your lecturers will as well. Who cares if the origins of your play can be traced back to the early Grecian plays of Aeschylus? Don't try to second-guess your lecturer's tastes and predilections. Chances are you'll have to produce an objective account of your writing process or a similar evaluation. That's your moment to put your academic skills into practice. So don't treat this as an opportunity to prove just how much academic knowledge you've gleaned so far on your course – it's a chance to show how good a writer you are. I've read a lot of university playwriting assignments and I can't tell you how depressing it is to see a germ of a good idea struggling to overcome the desire to impress.

I'm not sure that the delineation between 'academic' and 'creative' is ever laid down clearly enough. You have a fantastic opportunity to write a play in a protected environment. Think of your relationship with your course tutor as that between playwright and literary manager. If you have an inkling that you would like to write professionally, let your tutor know. There's nothing more encouraging for an academic than the discovery that one of their students has completely engaged with the course, and isn't simply going through the motions in order to graduate. At university I received a lot of support from my playwriting tutor, who was directly responsible for my first production at the Edinburgh Fringe Festival. You may be lucky enough to find that your tutor is also happy to read future plays – it's certainly worth trying to cultivate a friendship here.

Student theatre

Theatre festivals can still be a good bet for budding or emerging playwrights hoping to get their work seen – in particular, the National Student Drama Festival and the Edinburgh Fringe. Of course, it's all a bit of a lottery with so many productions vying for attention. It can also be very expensive to mount productions in Edinburgh, or at other international theatre festivals. You must be prepared to make a loss.

When I first took a play up to Edinburgh I was convinced I was about to hit the big time. I was so confident I'd even chosen a swanky pair of tartan trousers to mark the occasion. I was cruelly disappointed. Sometimes the cast outnumbered audience members three to one, and that was after reasonable reviews. However, I have known writers who've languished in relative obscurity until they've taken a play to Edinburgh.

Many theatres will send scouts to the Edinburgh Festival so get in touch with your local theatre, or any other companies you may have had a relationship with, no matter how fleeting. Let them know where your play is being performed and any other relevant details.

If you are fortunate enough to be reviewed, and even more fortunate to discover that the reviews are positive, you potentially have a bargaining chip at your disposal.

How should I lay out my script?

To be honest, there's no industry-approved layout for play scripts. It tends to vary from writer to writer, or perhaps more accurately from publisher to publisher. As a rule of thumb, it's not a bad idea to go into your local bookshop or library and flick through published plays until you find a layout that looks good to you. It's always useful to see how other writers set out their scripts. Look at scripts published by Nick Hern Books, Oberon, Faber or Methuen, for example. Some playwrights have started to lay out their stage plays as they would a film screenplay. Call me old-fashioned, but I rather like stage plays to *look* like stage plays on the page.

Are there any playwriting packages for my computer, or should I just use Word?

Although there are computer packages available that will help you to format your scripts, formatting is far less prescriptive for the theatre than it is for film, TV or radio. If you've convinced yourself that you can't put pen to paper until you can afford to buy this sort of software, you're mistaken.

Resist the temptation to tie everything up with a great big bow

You're inevitably finding some way to tie up the disparate (or not so disparate) plot strands of your play. But don't pander to your audience by giving them what you *think* they want or need. Give them what's right for the *play*.

Can you imagine a worse time to lose your audience than at the very end of your play? Situations are often resolved, but in life we rarely reach anything that we can describe as a clear conclusion.

Often an abrupt and violent act can be the least satisfying way of reaching a dramatic climax:

- A gun is fired
- A character is killed
- A character commits suicide

There's a disconcerting and unsatisfactory slamming on of the brakes – something is artificially thrown into the mix to help provide a definitive full stop to the action. It always makes me think of the stories I had to write in school as a child, when I ran out of ideas and so concluded the tale when the protagonist awoke to discover 'it had all been a dream'.

Life doesn't end happily or unhappily. It just ends. It all boils down to one essential truth; nothing in life is ever simple.

Time to catch up

Make yourself a cup of tea/coffee/alternative beverage, sit down and take stock. Good. Are you sitting comfortably?

So how are you getting on? Where are you with your script? Has it been plain sailing, or are you up a creek without the proverbial paddle?

I'm halfway through my play and I'm stuck. Help!

It really is very easy to lose the plot, both literally and metaphorically. This is the point where many people lose confidence and contemplate throwing in the towel. But take heart.

In all probability the novelty has worn off, that's all. You're so familiar with what you initially thought was a good idea that you begin to doubt every word you write. That doesn't necessarily mean, however, that you are writing a hopeless play. You may well be writing a very good play, but how will you know until you finish it?

It's time to look at your work through fresh eyes

But what happens when you come back to your work with a more objective and critical eye? How do we switch from creator to editor? Suddenly, it's no longer about quantity but quality as you start going back through your script to remove the scaffolding.

We've all been there, reading back through a script and thinking 'why did I write that?' or, worse still, 'I don't even *remember* writing that'. But don't despair. You've come too far to give up now.

Before you read back through the script, remind yourself why you wanted to tell this story in the first place. Condense this into a single sentence and commit it to paper. Now, put that piece of paper to one side.

Now re-read your script

Don't take notes at this point. Read the script as if you're coming to it for the very first time. Imagine for a moment that you were *not* the writer of this play. What story is the playwright telling? Again, crystallize this into a single sentence and write it on a separate piece of paper.

Once you've finished reading the script, look back at your two sentences. Be honest with yourself. Is this the script you set out to write? Are the two sentences essentially the same, or is there a divergence here?

We all make shifts and adjustments as we're writing. It's possible that you are now telling a better story than you'd originally imagined. But if you're not happy, decide what you need to do in order to return to your original idea.

Re-read your script, but this time do take notes as you go along. The important thing is to be honest with yourself. If you have a concern, try not to sweep it under the carpet: meet the problems head on.

It's easy to get bogged down in a morass of words so it can be helpful to think in more three-dimensional terms. I'll often print out a scene and lay the pages on the floor in front of me. It can provide a far better sense of the overall shape of a scene than reading one page at a time on a computer screen.

It's always important to tell the story *you* want to tell. Don't tell the story you think *other people* want you to tell.

How do I know when my play's finished? Someone told me it's sometimes better to send an unformed idea you're really passionate about to a theatre, rather than something you've worked and worked on

How can we determine when a draft is finished? This is another of those 'how long is a piece of string?' questions. Is a script *ever* truly finished? Many writers tinker with their scripts after the first production, some plays remain in a permanent state of development, re-worked after every subsequent production. It can become an obsessive process. But at some point, you need to take the plunge – and only you can decide when that time has arrived.

I'm worried that my play still isn't ready to send out, but I don't know how to make the script any better. What do I do?

Is your play really not ready to send out, or have you convinced yourself of the fact as a defence mechanism? Sometimes you have to take a risk. If a script remains on your desk gathering dust it's no good to anybody. So don't let the grass grow beneath your feet. Look back over the script once more. Is it possible to crank up the tension? If you can see an obvious way of improving your play, then improve it. Be strict with yourself – don't simply settle for 'OK'.

Either way, don't leave the script lying around. What's the worst that can happen?

Can I send a script out to lots of theatres at the same time? Can I email it?

To help keep track of where you are it might be sensible to send your script out in batches. It's worth sending it out to three or four theatres, just to test the water.

Always have a spare printer ink cartridge tucked away at the back of a drawer. If possible, buy several at a time so there's never any danger of running out.

I've got a hunch that many more people are sending in unsolicited play scripts than might have been the case ten or fifteen years ago. Once again it's 'cool' to be a playwright, and many hundreds of people are jostling in line to become the next West End or Broadway sensation. Only ever email a script to a theatre if you've been expressly asked to do so.

Do different theatres have a certain sort of play they like?

It can be difficult to predict a theatre's specific tastes and predilections. Again, a little research can help to cast light on this. Most theatres list current and recent productions on their websites and a little bit of internet research should help to fill in gaps in your knowledge. Of course, there's no better form of research than going to the theatre and watching plays. If a production of a new play seems to be attracting a buzz, do all you can to get tickets. Many plays are taken on regional tour, so even if you don't live in the teeming metropolis, it's no excuse not to go to the theatre.

Why not become a friend of your local theatre? Attend post-show discussions – or go on a backstage tour (check online, many theatres will list this on their website). This is a good way to see behind the scenes, and gain insight into the running of the theatre.

The National Theatre in London, for example, runs back-stage tours most days of the week (although it might be sensible to book in advance). It's a brilliant opportunity to study at first hand what makes a theatre tick. Take every opportunity you can to get a feel for your craft. Even sitting in an empty theatre can be a worthwhile experience, soaking up all the creative energy that lingers in such places by a process of osmosis.

Even if you can't get to the theatre as much as you'd like, trade papers such as *The Stage* and *Theatre Record* can give a wide-ranging impression of what's on. Most weekend supplements list theatre productions in London and further afield.

How many new scripts are submitted to UK theatres each year?

The Traverse Theatre in Edinburgh receives 450 scripts a year. The Royal Court in London gets 3,000 scripts and offers to give feedback on each one. Manchester Royal Exchange receives between 450–500 scripts, but will only read one script from a writer each year. The National Theatre receives 1,500 scripts a year, but will not give feedback on plays that it is not interested in developing.

Don't be put off by statistics. Lots of theatres quote the number of scripts they might receive in an average year. What they don't say is how many of these scripts are actually any good. Probably a tiny percentage. So take heart.

How many people should I show my play to before sending it off somewhere?

Obviously you're not being judged on your literacy skills, but do check back through your script for slips in spelling, punctuation and grammar. If you're in doubt, get somebody to look over it for you. My mother used to check mine through for me. It was incredible the number of things I usually missed – and continue to miss.

As far as constructive criticism is concerned, be careful. If you give the script to six different people to read you could well end up with six different opinions and all of them conflicting. It's hard enough taking one person's feedback on board. It's a nightmare trying to digest feedback from half a dozen people. We all need support and encouragement, but if you can hold off looking for a second opinion until you've finished your first draft, so much the better.

I get by with a little help from my friends ...

Nature, as science has taught us, abhors a vacuum. A network of support is really helpful, or, as a friend of mine describes it, 'finding a tribe of fellow writers'. As a therapist will turn to another therapist to offload, so too a playwright needs a confidante/confessor. Knowing that you can pick up the phone and whinge for half an hour can be the release you so desperately need in times of trouble. A problem shared is a problem halved and all that.

If I didn't have a friend within easy reach at the end of the phone I would probably have gone insane long ago.

Again, if you lack faith in your spelling and punctuation, ask a trusted friend to comb through the script for you. I think it's always a good idea to have a second pair of eyes looking through a script before you send it off. If nothing else, it can go some way to putting your mind at rest. However, don't let yourself be fobbed off with unequivocal praise (tempting though it may be to rest on your laurels, and accept the well-meaning pronouncement that your script is undoubtedly the best thing since sliced bread, or Pinter).

Hide the script away for a fortnight!

There's a lot to be said for pushing the finished script to one side and forgetting about it for a couple of weeks. There's an awful legitimacy to the printed word. It's very easy to look at a printed script and miss any number of errors. Put the script in a drawer, ideally under lock and key, and come back to it later. At all costs, resist the temptation to begin tinkering with your script. The more distance you can place between yourself and the completed draft of your play, the better. Again, learn to cultivate an objective eye.

How can I tell if my lines are working?

Read the script aloud. This may sound obvious, but try it. Sometimes I've read through lines of dialogue that suddenly seem almost impossible to deliver.

If you can, try to assemble a group of people to read the script aloud for you. Turn it into a social occasion – I do. I'll buy a couple of bottles of wine, lay on some nibbles, and invite a group of friends to read through my script for me (it's often been my experience that the better the nibbles and wine, the better the reading will be). It's a way of creating distance between yourself and the script.

Record the reading if you want; you can always listen back to any problematic sections of the script later on.

Less is more

I hate having to fall back on truisms, but 'less is more'. Many plays could be vastly improved by cutting the first five to ten pages of dialogue. This may seem a rather arbitrary comment, but often these first few pages are thick with set-up, which just gets in the way of the play and could be discarded without causing any harm at all. Plunge straight into a scene – make the audience work to understand what's going on. Strip back, clear the dead wood. Be careful though, as it is possible to trim a script back to such an extent that the characters are practically reduced to robots, performing very specific functions. If a section of dialogue is revealing of character, then it probably isn't padding and doesn't need to be cut away.

I used to find cutting a truly depressing enterprise. It seemed a counter-creative act – to destroy rather than create. It seems entirely contrary to every writerly instinct. But actually it's often a really liberating experience. Think of yourself as an archaeologist excavating, digging back the layers of earth to reveal the hidden treasures beneath the surface.

OK, so grab a fluorescent marker or a red pen, and look back through the first few pages of your script. What can you take out without damaging the integrity of the writing? You're not going to do anything as brutal as cutting (yet). There's always something freeing about taking out biros and fluorescent markers and scribbling all over a script. As soon as you feel happy with your proposed cuts, try taking out the chunk of text. Remember, anything you feel unhappy about removing can be replaced at the click of a button.

I went to see a play and it was rubbish! Now I feel thoroughly disheartened. Is it worth carrying on when people are happy to put on rubbish plays like this?

People don't deliberately decide to stage a play that they think is terrible. What would be the point? 'But I can write rubbish plays too' is not a good argument. It's always a question of subjective taste, and one man's meat is another man's poison. Don't be disheartened – think of it as throwing down the gauntlet. Go away and work hard to prove that you can write a better play.

What do they mean when they talk about 'finding your voice'?

A lot of writers find it difficult to trust in their own view of the world so it's hardly surprising that many plays are written in a clearly identifiable mould. We don't write in a vacuum – we can't help but be influenced by the work of other writers. That said, 'imitation is the sincerest form of flattery' is an argument that doesn't hold water here. Learn from the masters, but don't try to copy them. If you attempt to emulate the work of more established writers you lose the very thing that potentially makes your work unique – your own voice.

With many first plays it's all too easy to identify the 'parent' of the play. Countless scripts land on a literary manager's desk each day that owe much to Pinter, Ayckbourn, Stoppard, *et al*. If *you* know it, a literary manager will certainly know it as well.

Trust in your own worldview, even if it takes a bit of time to make that adjustment.

Read and re-read your script

Fight the temptation to send off your script the moment you've completed work on it. You'll rarely have an opportunity to re-submit a script once it's been rejected. Be honest with yourself – if you're not happy with the script, don't send it out. Think about the impression you're attempting to make.

To err is not divine

I do read plays occasionally that have clearly not been checked for spelling errors. Be careful of 'false friends' – those words that a computer spellchecker will not pick up. The word is correctly spelt, but it's being used in the wrong context (years ago I typed in Ovaltine, and the computer suggested 'ovulating').

A spelling error on the first page of the script smacks of laziness. You may think this never happens but, trust me, it does. On one memorable occasion not only was there a spelling error on page one, the very first word was spelt incorrectly – and that was the title of the play.

Avoiding the obvious pitfalls

There are a number of 'mistakes' that can quickly betray the fact that a writer is at an early stage in their playwriting career. Never, ever, submit a handwritten script. I even think a script written on a manual typewriter will raise eyebrows in this day and age. On the other hand, don't spend too much time and money on presentation. I used to make sure my scripts were professionally bound before I sent them off. Smart as it may have looked, it made not one iota of difference. It could also be argued that a bound script actually takes up extra space on a literary manager's shelves. Imagine what would happen if everybody submitted bound scripts – it would be a disaster. Shelf units would be buckling in every theatre in the land. There's also the nagging suspicion that the fanciness of the binding may be compensating for deficiencies in the script.

Imagine you've sent in your script. A literary manager picks up the script, turns to the first page, and encounters a table of contents. Already the writer has communicated the fact that they've probably never read a published play text. Scripts *never* include a table of contents.

Also, don't feel that you have to provide detailed character biographies. Present your play as simply as possible. Actually, the more extraneous material you include, the more damningly you mark yourself out as an inexperienced writer. Don't include CDs of music you want played during the production, or set designs you've knocked up with a friend; don't highlight characters' names in different colours. I've seen all these things happen in the past, and ultimately it just gets in the way.

If you don't have an agent, put your own address and contact telephone number in the bottom left-hand corner of the cover page as scripts often become separated from their cover letters. Do number your pages. Sometimes it's necessary for a theatre to photocopy a script to pass on to readers – it's much more difficult reassembling a script that hasn't been numbered!

So, in short, submit a clean, numbered and neatly printed script. Anything else is excess baggage.

Writing a cover letter

You don't have to make yourself interesting in order for people to pay attention to your script. People sometimes try to be hysterically funny in their cover letters. I'll be honest, it rarely works. If you read back over your letter and cringe, then you're one of those people.

Confidence is never a bad thing, arrogance always is. Keep your letter succinct and to the point. If you've already had plays produced, do mention this briefly in your cover letter.

Research your market

How would you feel if a letter arrived through your post box addressed 'dear homeowner'? Your first instinct is probably to pick up the offending literature and pop it in the recycling bin. Why should theatres feel any differently?

Why do you want this theatre to produce your play? If you can't answer that question, why are you sending them your script? Think of it as a targeted campaign. Only send your script to theatres you'd be happy working with.

Too often a playwright will pick up a theatre directory and send out their play indiscriminately. This scattershot approach is perhaps not the most sensible way of working and will do little to endear you to a literary manager.

The *Writers' & Artists' Yearbook* is a mine of information, as is the *British Theatre Directory*. But information can quickly become outdated. It's worth contacting the theatre directly to check who a script should be addressed to. Or check online. Many theatre companies list submission details on their websites.

What happens next?

There is often a failure to understand what happens after the play is sent off to a theatre company. If the script has been written with alacrity, there is sometimes a misguided belief that the script will be read with the same energy and enthusiasm. If only this were the case.

For starters, it may take a couple of days for your script to reach its destination. The package may be opened immediately, but chances are the script will be carefully placed on an already toppling slush pile. It may of course be passed on to one of the literary department's readers, who will read the script and provide a short written report which will be passed back to the theatre's literary manager. More time will pass. Often the theatre will hold regular meetings with their script readers, during which your play will possibly be discussed. Perhaps the reader loved your script – what then? Unfortunately, even if the script reader is passionate about your play, it's no guarantee that this enthusiasm will translate into a production. There are always too many plays competing for too few slots.

Expect the worst, hope for the best

I always used to send out scripts with a stamped addressed jiffy bag for return. This process is a great leveller. There's nothing worse than the soft, padded thud of a jiffy bag dropping through the letterbox at breakfast time to ruin a day. Understandably, a lot of would-be writers find the constant rejection impossible to bear. But it *is* a process that most writers have to go through. You're not alone. Look at it this way – how could you possibly know exactly what it is that a theatre is looking for? It's knowledge that you'll gain over time. You see? Even rejection serves a purpose.

What is a literary manager looking for?

Essentially, I think that all good literary managers are looking for that precious commodity – a diamond in the rough. Again, they will be looking for an original 'voice' – the writer's own, specific take on the world around them. But very few literary managers would expect a perfect and production-ready script to land on their desks.

Some writers are so hamstrung by the need to attain perfection that they never feel ready to send their work out into the world. That's not to say you shouldn't polish your work as much as possible, but there does come a point where you must down tools and offer up your script. To a literary manager, the indication that a writer is rigorous in their work is a promising sign. Sometimes, however, if a script has been over-polished, it can be more difficult to offer the writer feedback: more difficult, in fact, to sort out the play.

It's not just publishers who get lumbered with a slush pile

Don't expect anything to happen overnight. It's way too easy to tell a writer to sit back and be patient, but when a play has been your all-consuming passion for months on end, patience is probably the furthest thing from your mind. Think how much worse it might be if you received a response by return. Trust in the fact that the process takes as long as it takes.

Possible response number one: your script is rejected

It can be extremely frustrating to receive a rejection letter that fails to detail the reasons why your play has been rejected. Don't expect detailed critical feedback on your script, although some theatres make a point of doing just that. Sometimes writers are apt to become a little cynical, and question whether their play has been read at all. Trust me, it will have been. You might be lucky enough to receive a one-page play report, explaining why it was turned down. This can be extremely helpful. Although, if you're anything like me, you probably find it hard to see the silver lining in any passing cloud.

None of us likes rejection. But here's something to bear in mind:

> Even good plays get turned down.

Quite apart from the fact that every response to a play is subjective, there are two main reasons why a strong play may be turned down:

1 Many theatres programme a long time in advance (sometimes several years in advance). It might be that your play has such a contemporary theme that it may age very quickly and seem dated by the time a pro-gramming slot opens up.
2 The theatre may have a glut of their own commissioned plays which need to be programmed before they can consider programming new plays.

Plays are rejected for many different reasons and, surprisingly, quality is only one of those reasons. I've read beautifully written scripts that have been turned down for practical (normally budgetary) considerations, which are no reflection on the obvious quality of the writing. A rejection is not necessarily a value judgement of your play. Don't dwell on things. After all, if you don't know the reason the play was turned down, why accept responsibility?

Try to take rejection on the chin. Trust me, you'll feel better for it the next day. But try to bear in mind that if your play has been turned down, it may only be on the basis of one person's opinion.

Many plays have been rejected by one theatre only to be picked up by another, produced and lauded to the hilt.

When do things stop being right and wrong and become a matter of taste?

Do you like every play you watch? Of course not. We don't all read the same books, so why would we want to watch the same plays? If a theatre rejects your play – that's it, move on. Trust me, there's nothing to be gained from writing back to the theatre and demanding that they explain *why* they turned down the script.

Remember, a rejection marks the end of your correspondence with the theatre (for that play at least).

'Writing is not a profession but a vocation of unhappiness.'

Georges Simenon

You do need to be resilient. If one rejection letter is enough to send you scurrying into a corner to lick your wounds, you have to ask yourself if you're tough enough to cope with the slew of rejections you will inevitably have to contend with in the years to come. Take heart, most writers have had to deal with rejection at some point. Unfortunately, it's not a part of the job that gets easier over time – although the early stabbing pains of rejection are often replaced by a duller, less exquisite pain. If more of your work is being sold than rejected, this is the medicine to treat the pain. But no writer is immune to rejection, especially early in their career.

OK, then, there's another moment of brutal honesty coming up, so prepare yourself:

YOU WOULD BE SPECTACULARLY FORTUNATE TO FIND THAT YOUR FIRST SCRIPT IS PICKED UP AND PRODUCED

This may seem a slightly negative thought to bear in mind, but it's an honest one. I'd be shirking my responsibility if I didn't tell you. Think of your first script as a calling card, an apprentice piece. If the play doesn't get produced but it *does* get you noticed, then it has served its purpose. If it gets noticed *and* produced, you're in profit. Nothing happened with my first script. So I started work on a new play. You *need* to be tenacious. It's often the case that as one door closes another opens.

I'm worried that somebody will steal my idea

This is a perennial chestnut. A writer will submit a script to the tender mercies of a literary department, only to find that their play is rejected. Then, horror of horrors, the following year the theatre in question will produce a play with eerie similarities to the script they turned down. Believe me, it's nothing but a coincidence. It's not a literary manager's job to steal ideas.

The theatre's decision is final

If your work is rejected, don't enter into protracted correspondence with the theatre in question. Trust me – they will not appreciate your tenacity. They won't have grudging respect for your do-or-die attitude. This sort of behaviour only marks you out as a maniac. And guess what? Chances are your next play will be rejected as well.

I was once sent a package (passed on by a puckish literary manager friend of mine) containing a painfully drawn-out correspondence between a disgruntled playwright and a leading regional rep. The theatre in question behaved with an almost saintly equanimity, the playwright did not. There are cringe-making stories of writers haranguing literary managers and artistic directors. I once heard of a literary manager who was in hospital with a broken leg, who was surprised by a visit from a playwright. But did he bring grapes or Lucozade for the ailing literary manager? No, he did not. He brought a script. Now that's a captive audience.

I spoke to one literary manager who was informed that an irate playwright was waiting for him at Stage Door with a baseball bat. Threats of actual bodily harm are not only poor form, they're also illegal. The blind pursuit of success is one thing. But please, do keep some perspective.

I don't want to sound cruel, but I'll be honest. People sit around and discuss these things. They compare notes on the bizarre and surreal things they've just read. It's human nature. A director friend of mine used to keep a file of terrible CVs, including an actress who claimed to have spent time working in a French 'brassiere'.

Who reads my script?

If you have begun to forge a relationship with a theatre, the chances are it will speed up the response time to any work you submit. Often the script will be read by the literary manager. But remember how overworked they are and don't chase them unless months have elapsed without hearing anything.

I realized once that I still hadn't had a response six years after I'd sent out a play to one theatre. That's probably the point where you can dash off a letter to find out what's become of your script.

I have heard of a commission coming to fruition months after the playwright sent in their script, which was later discovered languishing behind a radiator.

Occasionally a writer will be told that although their play is not suitable, the literary manager would be interested in reading their next script. I always think this is a very positive response, so don't feel that you're being fobbed off with platitudes. If a theatre offered optimistic rejection letters to every playwright, they'd be courting disaster with the inevitable slew of scripts that would land on their desks.

Response number two: the theatre invites you in for a meeting

If a theatre is interested in your writing, you may be invited in for a chat. A meeting with the literary manager or artistic director may not lead to a commission, but what it does give you is the opportunity to have a face-to-face conversation with someone in the know. And rest assured, they must have seen promise in your writing or you wouldn't have been invited in. It simply wouldn't be worth their while. Remember, as a wise friend of mine once said, good things can come out of a cup of coffee.

Do prepare for the meeting. A question you will almost certainly be asked is: 'So, what productions have you seen here recently?'

Obviously, if your answer is 'none', it does close off a possible avenue of conversation. If you haven't been able to watch any recent productions at the theatre, look online. At least you should be able to get a sense of the work they've been producing.

If you've been invited in for a meeting on the strength of your script, it's quite possible you'll be asked if you have any other ideas in mind. It's never a bad idea to have two or three ideas up your sleeve. Who knows, it may be that one of these ideas is of interest.

If a literary manager has engaged with your play, it's more than likely he or she will want to know more about you. This is more to do with placing your play in some sort of biographical context than out-and-out nosiness (although sometimes it really is intriguing to place a play with a face). As you well know, a script doesn't arrive fully formed on the page. In many respects, it is an extension of you, the playwright. The location, characters and dramatic thrust of your play may well have been shaped by your own personal experiences.

If you are a more experienced playwright, a literary manager will often ask whether you are working on any other commissions. Deep down they're almost certainly trying to work out whether you would view a commission for their theatre as your main priority.

What happens if I get a commission?

The relief of finally being offered a commission can be a bit of an anticlimax. You tend to feel so tired and battered by the series of rejections that have led you to this point that you'd rather curl up in a ball and weep than race out to paint the town red.

What you should expect depends vastly on the theatre that has commissioned you. In most cases a theatre will ask what you would like to write. The reason for this is a simple one. A writer will almost always find they produce their best work if the idea comes from their own imagination. Writing someone else's idea often undermines the creative process.

The 'up' side to a commission

If a theatre has invested in a commission, they're more likely to see the resulting play through to production. The fact that they commissioned you in the first place is a firm indication that they see you as a writer of promise.

Some theatres will over-commission and cherry-pick the best-of-the-best, although this perhaps occurs far less frequently than paranoid gossip might suggest.

It's rare for a commission to be offered which provides the playwright with an entirely free hand. There are normally certain practical considerations that need to be taken into account. The chief consideration is usually cast size. It's unlikely that you'll be commissioned without a discussion about how many actors your play will require. It's unusual for a theatre to commission a large-cast play, but it does (occasionally) still happen.

Smaller companies may have certain practical considerations in mind when they commission a play. If the production is going to be taken on tour, the set, props, costumes (and cast) may have to be packed into the back of a van at the end of the night to be driven on to the next venue.

Help! I've been asked for a synopsis

A successful meeting at a theatre might result in you being asked to submit a synopsis – a potted outline of a play you want to write.

In many respects, the synopsis is as useful for you as it is for a literary manager and artistic director. It gives you an opportunity to crystallize your idea as you commit it to paper.

Don't give everything away and do allow yourself room for the idea to develop. In fact, the longer the synopsis, the more difficult it can be to pin down the essence of the idea. It needn't be longer than a page.

And it's always something you can return to in the weeks and months ahead if you feel you've begun to stray too far from your original idea.

You won't be expected to write reams of plot, with exhaustive character back stories. It's not that sort of document. It's a statement of intent, rather than a hard-and-fast blueprint for your play. Think of it as a roadmap if you like and keep it short and snappy.

Until you sit down and start writing your play, it's impossible to tell exactly where the story might lead you – and that's as it should be. More often than not the resulting play will diverge considerably from the original outline. This is no bad thing and a theatre will rarely expect you to follow your synopsis to the letter.

If you find that your play is veering a long way from the original commission idea, it's not a bad idea to keep the theatre up to speed. There are certain practical considerations you should bear in mind. For example, if you suggested your play was going to be a two-hander and you've ended up with a cast of six, this may not go down too well.

Response number three: they like my play but want me to make changes

Try to read through the draft without making a single note or alteration. View the play as a whole. I can't tell you the number of times I've furiously scribbled in a line only to discover that I've already written exactly the same line a page or two later – or cut out a line that I've immediately had to reinstate.

'Plays are not written, but re-written.'

There is a real 'art' to editing and revising a script, and it's an art that's learnt with time and experience. Often a bit of distance will help you to clear your head. But too much distance can be counterproductive. The longer you leave it before you return to the play, the harder it will be to get back into it.

Also, you'll quite possibly discover that your writing style changes over the months and years – sometimes in a barely perceptible way, but at times it can shift to such an extent that it feels as though you're returning to someone else's play.

So strike while the iron's hot – or at least lukewarm. I've rarely regretted tackling a new draft straight away.

'There are three basic human instincts. Food, reproduction of the species, and the desire to edit someone else's play.'

Anon

If there's anything that still needs clarification, do drop the theatre an email or pick up the phone. Don't forget, this is a collaborative process. You're not being tested. Ultimately you're working together towards the same goal – the production of your play.

Some literary managers will be more 'hands on' than others, but don't rely on anyone else to motivate you. You won't have a phone call from the literary manager every week to prod you and see how you're getting on. You'll be left to your own devices. It's not lack of interest, you're just being given space to go away and write your play. If you need to have your hand held every step of the way, you may find it an uphill struggle.

Most of the time communication between a playwright and a theatre is conducted by telephone and email. Over time you'll discover the best approach for you. As my friend the literary manager says:

'It's about creating the environment in which people can write the best play they can and tailor-making what support the writer needs.'

Become a thorough note-taker

When you've had a script meeting at your commissioning theatre it is sometimes useful to turn the new draft around as quickly as possible, while the literary manager or artistic director's thoughts and observations are still fresh in your mind. I always go home and type up my notes after a meeting. In the past I have left it for days before doing this, then been completely unable to decipher my own hand-writing. These notes are useful to have close to hand as you start work on the new draft of the script.

Unlike publishing, when a book editor will probably scribble notes all over your manuscript, it's unlikely that this will happen with a play text. Without these little 'cues' or hints scribbled in the margin of your script, you do need to become a thorough note-taker, just to make certain that you are grasping the nettle when a literary manager or director talks through their notes with you. By now the literary manager will know the play very well. And what they will have, that you may not, is a certain amount of detachment and a rather more objective overview. To put it another way – the literary manager will be reading the script as an audience will be watching it.

How many drafts will it take?

One, two … twelve? Who knows? I'll be honest with you, that is one of the frustrations of the job; taking your first step when the play is commissioned, but having little or no idea how long the journey will be. And it can be immensely frustrating to get to the stage where it feels as though you're dotting every 'i' and crossing every 't' and the theatre has still not committed to a firm production date.

There can't be many more destructive forces for a writer than this crushing sense of inertia. Sometimes an agent might wade in at this point and apply a certain amount of gentle pressure to get a decision from the theatre in question. A 'no' is often kinder than a 'maybe'.

I do think committing to production can sometimes provide the necessary shove a playwright needs to speed them through the final drafts of a script. There's nothing like a looming start date for rehearsals to focus the mind!

How long will I wait to hear back from the theatre?

You can expect the response time to be considerably quicker than if you've sent in an unsolicited script, but again this all depends on the size of the theatre. It's extremely unlikely that the script will be farmed out to a freelance script reader, and will almost certainly be read by the literary manager, or even the artistic director (or both).

How do I word a contract, or will the theatre do that for me?

Most theatres will send you, or your agent, a standard contract. There will almost certainly be a tiered payment system, based on 'actors' working hours', the template for which will have been approved by the Writers' Guild of Great Britain and the Society of Authors. It offers a degree of protection for playwrights whether or not they are members of these organizations.

It's sound business sense to read through the contract, even if you are represented by an agent.

'Don't believe anything until you see it in black and white.'

If there's anything you find confusing, do ask for advice. It is your fundamental right.

It's my personal maxim that anything that sounds too good to be true *is* too good to be true.

How will I be paid?

If you're writing to commission, it's likely that you'll be paid in three instalments. Half of the total sum will be released on signature of the contract. A further quarter of the total sum will be paid on delivery of the first draft of the script. The final quarter of the commission fee will be released on acceptance of the script for production. The commission is a non-returnable advance against royalties. And non-returnable means just that. You won't have to repay the money if the theatre is ultimately unable to produce your play. It will normally take about a week for the money to clear into your account after your agent has received payment. In most cases money will be transferred as an electronic BACS payment. Of course, if you do not have an agent you will be paid directly by the theatre.

As a wise man once advised me, 'draw a weekly wage'. This is excellent financial advice, and I've never listened to a word of it. If I lived according to my means, I'd never eat. The natural inclination (or mine, anyway) is to go out and shop, but it really is important to pace yourself. It's impossible to tell quite how long that commission fee will have to sustain you. All well and good if you're able to write your play, finish it, and have it accepted for production in a few short months. But what if it takes eighteen months or two years to work the script up to a production-ready draft?

I have known instances when a theatre has advanced the acceptance fee to help a writer out when finances are tight. This is incredibly generous behaviour, and happens rarely. It happens so rarely, I wonder why I am even writing this.

Some writers prefer not to write to commission. If money

were no obstacle, this is probably the way most playwrights would choose to work.

I wake up thankful every day that I'm able to draw a living from writing. Any right-thinking writer does.

As already discussed, payment for a commission will normally be in line with Writers' Guild and TMA (Theatrical Management Association) guidelines. However, there are some slightly more unscrupulous companies who clearly believe that writers should be so pathetically grateful for any scraps thrown their way that they will be only too happy to accept a paltry commission. Quite frankly, there are some theatres that should know better. If it's clear that the commissioning company can't afford to pay more than a couple of hundred pounds for a script and you're happy to go along with this, then fair enough.

I have seen a sinister strategy in operation, where writers are invited to tender for a possible commission without any indication of how much the commission fee will be. This is a pretty mean trick. Creativity isn't enough to feed the soul – sandwiches are also good. As they say, if you pay peanuts you get monkeys. But at least the monkeys would be *fed*.

The first time I was ever paid to write I received a very small commission indeed. But I was working with a director and production company that I trusted, and I knew that they had worked very hard to scrape together the money to pay me.

Generally speaking, I would say 'playwright beware!' If you take on the commission, but find you don't have enough money to keep body and soul together, you only have yourself to blame. Alas, money is the fuel that stokes the fire of a writer's imagination.

Getting an agent

An agent's choice to represent you may be even more subjective than a theatre's decision to produce your play. If an agent doesn't feel passionately enthusiastic about your writing, it will be difficult for him to sell your work. It has been said that an agent needs to feel you stand a chance of raking in at least £10,000 a year in order for it to be worth his while to offer representation. Agents don't take on clients because of some warm-and-fuzzy desire to protect and nurture playwrights as an act of charity. This isn't patronage, it's representation. Again, you do have to bear in mind that this is a business relationship.

Do I need an agent? If so, how do I approach one?

This may seem an obvious piece of advice, but there's little point in approaching an agent unless you've written a play. I didn't get an agent until after I had my first play produced. Obviously, having had the play produced made it easier to get an agent. But even then it took almost a year (my best friend opened a bottle of champagne to celebrate).

I think there may actually be a benefit to waiting until you have secured a production of your play before looking for an agent. For one reason, it's an indication that you are already a bankable commodity. Don't make any decisions lightly. If all goes well this will be a relationship that will continue for many years – perhaps your entire writing career. If you're asked if you're meeting with other agents, be honest. You don't have to be secretive. An agent will appreciate that this is an important decision for you.

Sometimes an agent will only consider reading an unsolicited script if it has had an industry recommendation. If your play is being produced by a theatre it's well worth asking if they can recommend an agent.

But don't despair if no agent is forthcoming. With prose writing, a lot of publishers won't consider reading a manuscript unless it's submitted through an agent. Thankfully this usually isn't the case with playwriting. So act as your own agent until you secure professional representation.

What am I looking for in an agent?

Do you feel that the agent is enthusiastic about your work? Perhaps most importantly of all – do you *like* the agent? Again, this may seem an obvious question, but do you feel that this is a person you'd happily chat to on the phone? Find out as much as you can about the agency. Research online and talk to other writers you may know.

Don't be seduced by the length of the agent's client list. It can be tremendously flattering to think of your own name among a roll call of the great and the good, but does this suggest that the agent may not see you as a priority?

One thing an agent is most decidedly *not* is a personal manager. You still have the responsibility for directing your own career. An agent will certainly give you advice, but it is not their job to lead you by the nose.

I think a lot of writers sign with an agent, then sit back and wait for the offers of work to roll in. I'm sorry to disabuse you, but this will almost certainly never happen.

Matters financial

There's a lot to be said for seeking out an accountant who has experience of this specialist field. An agent may be able to suggest accountants, but remember they have no responsibility for handling your financial affairs beyond taking receipt of any monies owed, less agency commission.

Do remember to hang on to receipts. A lot of your expenses can be claimed when you submit your tax return. Books, stationery, travel expenses (to theatres, or for research trips) are all legitimate business expenses for a playwright. You can even claim office space.

As a commission can take a considerable amount of time to come to fruition, it's often possible to spread commission payments over a couple of years, leaving you with a less terrifying tax bill at the end of your financial year.

Back to the play: is another character really necessary?

It can be tempting to think that all you need is another character or two to sort things out. But hold on. Far from sorting things out, adding an extra character can often further complicate the problem. Don't forget, it's another mouth to feed, another character who will plead needily with you from somewhere inside your subconscious.

The more characters you have on stage, the more plates you have to juggle. And try not to add too many smaller parts – spare a thought for the poor actor who spends the entire first act stuck in his dressing room, drinking tea, completing the *Guardian* crossword and bitterly wishing he had an agent who could get him a part in both acts of a play. I'm not suggesting that you write your play juggling creativity and accountancy. However, plays cost money to produce – hold that thought at the back of your mind – now forget about it and get on and write your play.

How quickly will I be expected to deliver the first draft of the script?

The delivery date in the contract will almost certainly be based on your discussions with the theatre. Nobody's going to spring a delivery date on you – nobody's trying to catch you out. There's usually provision for the renegotiation of delivery dates.

Honesty is always the best policy

'I like deadlines. I like the whooshing noise they make as they pass me by.'

Douglas Adams

When I first started writing, I was still living at home. I had got so behind with a play that I hid whenever the theatre in question telephoned to find out how I was getting on. My mother, a scrupulously honest woman, made me stand outside so she could answer the telephone and truthfully say that I wasn't at home. This was terrible practice, and I hang my head in shame as I recall the memory.

Remember, it's a very small world. Literary managers talk to each other – notes are compared. It can easily get around that you're unreliable at delivering drafts. There's nothing wrong with being a perfectionist, many writers are. Perfectionism is only ever a problem if it inhibits delivery.

There may be occasions where you have to turn a script round quickly. It's easy to get caught up in the excitement of a commission, swept along on a tide of euphoria that leads you to make idiotic promises like 'I think I can probably get the first draft to you by the end of the month.' Stop and count to ten. Work out what other commitments you have and whether or not your proposed delivery date is a realistic one. Bear in mind how much research you may need to do before you can actually get down to the work of writing the play. The lure of money can do crazy things to people. Try not to let it do crazy things to you. Be practical about how long it will take you to write the first draft of your script.

Don't set yourself unrealistic goals

Sometimes you can be hit by an idea like a bolt from the blue. Some days you may find you've knocked out a couple of thousand words without breaking a sweat. Other days it may seem impossible to write more than a couple of hundred words. Ideas often develop slowly. Sometimes very slowly. It can take months or even years for everything to slot neatly into place.

Rome was not built in a day. But, even so, try not to let your momentum slip. If you do find yourself staring at a blank computer screen for hours on end and nothing's happening then stop and take a break. If it's not working for you, try a different approach. I like to think it was Victoria Wood (although I'm not certain it was) who once said 'always stop writing when you know you can write more'.

Essentially, there are two distinct types of playwright

First, there's the sort of writer that I envy – the type who gets up early, maintains reasonable office hours, then closes the office door behind them at 5.30. Second, there's a pale, sickly sort of dramatist who works through the night, battling to stay on top of an impending deadline.

I have to confess that I'm in the second group, although I'm trying very hard not to be. Even though I'm constantly vowing never to do it again, I do still find occasions when I have to work through the night to complete a draft. After a while I find myself entering a slightly hypnotic state, free from the interruptions of telephone calls and emails. I can soon get absolutely lost in the world of the play. P.G. Wodehouse once commented on the fact that a lot of writer friends who wrote through the night were beginning to die off. This could be a disincentive.

Be realistic and allow yourself enough time to complete your script. I would like to think I can turn around a play in six months. But then, there are lots of things I'd *like* to think. Six months can seem like an awfully long time if you say it quickly. But that's the thing about time, it does have a way of flying.

I've been very slow with commissions. I've been very quick with commissions. There's often no rhyme or reason to it. For unaccountable reasons some plays take longer to write than others. It's as simple or as complicated as that.

Strangely, there's no substantial difference between the work I've generated quickly, and the work I've slaved over. I've even got a hunch that the quicker written plays were the better for it. That said, it is far, far better to send in your script when you feel it's ready. A lot of writers feel compelled to meet their deadlines, even if it means sending in a draft that really isn't complete. This can be a dangerous approach.

It's incredibly easy to become demotivated. Just accept that everybody reaches this point, not just you. We all procrastinate and put things off. We want to be anywhere but behind our desks. You've never seen my house tidier than when a deadline looms. I don't just dust, I polish. I once locked myself away in a particularly gloomy hotel on Russell Square as I attempted to bash out the final draft of a script. From time to time my mobile would ring. I didn't answer. It was a bad hotel. The key to my room was attached to a long metal pole so I couldn't nick it. Yet in its grimly utilitarian way, it provided everything I needed to work. My spine had become gelatinous, and I found myself completely unable to talk to the theatre's artistic director in person. My agent kindly interceded on my behalf and everything was smoothed over. No grudges were held, the play did good box office and I walked away with a reasonable royalties cheque.

What does a dramaturg do?

To be honest, I even have trouble pronouncing the word. Is it drama-turg or drama-*turge*? Who knows?

Essentially, what a good dramaturg is doing is working out exactly what it is you're attempting to *do* with your play. He or she will help you to shape and refine your script within the parameters you've established from your first draft onwards. It's a position without glory. The midwife to the play. Rather like a script doctor for a screenplay.

A good dramaturg will push the writer to hone the play they set out to write. A bad dramaturg will push a playwright to create a very different script altogether.

How do I take back ownership of my play when it's been dramaturged to death?

As a literary manager friend of mine says: 'People who ask questions of the work are probably very good dramaturgs. If you're finding it difficult, that's probably bad dramaturgy.'

There's almost always room for negotiation. Sometimes confusions can easily be talked out. A theatre will naturally be keen to help encourage you to write the best play possible. Their input will be intended to help you and not to undermine your creative vision. But don't agree to changes simply to please.

I have found in the past that I've been bullied into making choices I just haven't agreed with. But I can honestly say that the path of least resistance will just leave you feeling frustrated in the long run.

Never feel bullied into making decisions that instinctively feel wrong. You're so close to the work that sometimes you might not be able to see the wood for the trees, but you can also point out nuances that others may overlook. It's not about forcing a square peg into a round hole. If you agree with the suggestions, fine. But don't feel obliged to change your script. Talk through any disagreements – clarify any points of confusion. Again, a good literary manager, dramaturg or director will encourage you to re-write your script within the perameters you've already established.

Time is precious, so don't be disheartened if discussion tends to dwell on the negative aspects of your play. It's simply economy of time. Literary managers are normally very overworked and it's often taken for granted that there's no need to dwell on the aspects of the play that are already working successfully. On occasions, a literary manager can discuss the flaws in a script with such enthusiastic (though well-intentioned) relish that it can massively inflate a problem so a writer goes home with absolutely no idea of how to begin the new draft.

I've got to make the play better, but it must still be my play

I used to be very anxious about other people suggesting ways in which I could re-write my play. I was worried that it would cease to be my play, that somehow I would lose ownership of the idea. The moment you take on board the creative feedback of other people it can feel like you're giving something away. But bear in mind that the feedback is a direct response to the play you've written. Without your play there would be no notes to give.

Nothing is ever perfect

The more you panic, the more difficult it is to write. If you're really struggling see if you can find a fellow writer who might be willing to offer critical feedback on your work. Mentoring can be fantastically helpful. When I started writing I was very lucky to receive guidance from a number of people. I would have been lost without this advice and support. My friend the literary manager again: '... there are some writers who want feedback after writing a single page. It depends on what they need.'

Some writers are happy to go away and write and re-write their plays with little external input.

Most playwrights need a certain amount of encouragement and advice at the beginning of their careers. It isn't a sign of weakness! Even the most established writers need advice and editorial support from time to time.

I used to worry about getting outside input, but it's important to learn to accept advice in the spirit in which it's given.

I've gone into more meetings than I can remember,

convinced that I'd reached the final draft of the script, only to be encouraged to go away and work on a new draft. Don't resist for the sake of resisting – you don't want to earn a reputation for being difficult. On the other hand, you don't want to be seen as a pushover. Actually, I don't think I've ever left a meeting thinking that a literary manager was wrong in asking me to have another bash at the script.

It can be tempting to junk everything and start from scratch, but don't throw the baby out with the bathwater. It's often best to work on the assumption that if it ain't broke, don't fix it.

Re-drafting can feel like one step forward and two steps back. I always like to find the smallest route in possible as I approach a new draft. Not so much a doorway back into the play, more of a cat flap. I start by putting the little things right. As a friend of mine once said, it's the verruca bath before you plunge back into the swimming pool. Trick yourself into getting back into the work; don't feel you've got to tackle the big problems first.

A literary manager once apologized for giving me a number of picky notes about spelling – I'd even inadvertently got a character's name wrong. 'Hope you don't mind these little alterations,' she said. I couldn't have been more grateful. Personally, I like starting with spelling mistakes and grammatical errors. It's a useful way to convince the conscious mind to get back to work.

Again, I find it difficult to work through notes in a chronological fashion. To leaf through page after page of corrections can be crushing to the spirit. So I might start halfway into the script, and bounce around from page to page. This may sound like cheating, but who's to say you can't work on the easiest-to-fix notes first? Have a go – I can almost guarantee you'll feel better for it!

Remind yourself what story you're trying to tell

Even a generally well-structured play can lose its thread. Remind yourself – what is the conflict? Sit down and go back through the play scene by scene. How clear is the story you're attempting to tell? Does each scene drive the story forward? If it doesn't, you're going to have to make some brutal decisions.

Struggling with Mr Messy – a cautionary tale

When I was a very small boy my nursery school thought it would be rollicking good fun for us all to sit down and draw a picture of Mr Messy (from the Mr Men books). Fundamentally, the task was a simple one. I had to pick up a red pen and scribble all over the page. But I couldn't do it. Something inside my brain shut down. A straightforward task had been turned into a difficult process (they even kept me in over break time, the swines!). As I write this now, I have a Mr Messy mug on my desk, symbolizing that I must never allow this to happen again.

All the feedback we've been given on our scripts, the positive and the negative, has a nasty way of condensing itself in the brain to form one deeply unhelpful thought: 'Just make the play better.' It's like a daunting New Year's Resolution: 'Be slim by February.'

I was given terrible advice once and it's haunted me ever since. I was told to tackle the major plot problems head on and forget about the smaller problems. Suddenly, the script became monumentally difficult.

Of course, some plays will need much more editorial input than others. But a good dramaturg should make you feel that it is a journey that is possible.

'A journey of a thousand miles begins with a single step.'

Confucius

'One usually dislikes a play while writing it, but afterwards it grows on one. Let others judge and make decisions.'

Anton Chekhov

How do I know if I'm improving my script? Or am I just making it worse?

If the prospect of making the script better wasn't terrifying enough, the fear of making it worse is even more paralysing.

There are certainly days when nothing seems to work properly. I've been having one of those days today. I'm working on draft seven of a script. There's one scene that needs to be re-thought completely, the rest of the play needs a bit of a polish up, but that's about it. But then the doubts creep in. Have I gone far enough with the re-write? Does it look as though I've tackled the notes head on? Even worse, there's the gnawing sense of gloom – that maybe all I've done is consolidate the problems.

So here's the trick, and it's a simple one – stop worrying and wade right on in. What can be written can also be unwritten, so if you don't feel you're progressing in the right direction you can always stop and start again.

Finishing the final draft

As I near the end of draft seven of my current play, I'm hoping that the end is in sight, but I can foresee at least another two drafts before the play is programmed for production.

If the first draft is about getting the play written, then the next few drafts are all about getting it right (or as right as possible). Unfortunately, you won't get paid for each draft you complete, and there could be any number of drafts between your first and your final drafts.

'But at what point will my play be accepted?' I hear you cry. This really is the million-dollar question.

You may feel your play is complete. It probably isn't.

A script shouldn't need a writer to hold its hand

With each successive draft you're cutting the strings between creator and creation, so that by the final draft, with luck, you no longer need to stand as advocate for your writing. Many times I've heard writers saying, 'Yes, but what you don't understand about this line/scene is …'. But a script needs to exist in its own right. What it doesn't need is you hanging round, holding its hand. The text has to speak for itself. You don't have to provide all the answers, but you do want to provide enough clues.

The re-drafting process can progress at a deathly crawl. But then, if playwriting were an easy job everybody would be doing it.

There inevitably comes a point, sooner rather than later, when you just can't see the word for the trees. The brain starts to wander and somehow the story can seem to get lost along the way. Sometimes I find it hard to see the light at the end of the tunnel. Sometimes I find it hard to see the tunnel. But I grope around blindly in the dark and I know that sooner or later I'll clutch on to stone. Have faith that eventually things will come right …

I would be lying if I told you to expect a specific number

of re-drafts before your play is ready for production. It can vary wildly. Most theatres will be reluctant to commit to production until the script is virtually ready to take straight into rehearsal – this is perhaps especially true for less experienced writers.

There may be a considerable hiatus after finishing the final draft of the play, often many months. But holes in the programme will occasionally open up – for a myriad number of reasons. If your play is ready and waiting to go, a performance date may well be bumped forward.

How long will I have to wait before my play is produced?

As my friend the literary manager says, a writer should:

> '... expect a really clear response about what is going to happen to their play. Is it going to go on? Is it going to be further developed? People aren't always clear.'

And this is a real problem because:

> 'When a writer asks whether or not a theatre will do their play, the second best answer is no.'

A lot of books on playwriting grind to a halt at the very point a play nears production. The actual production of a play is an aspect of playwriting that is frequently (and surprisingly) omitted from books on the subject. Consequently, new writers often wind up on the first day of rehearsals with little idea of what to expect. Yet scripts often go through their most important stages of development in the rehearsal process. To me, this is the point where it starts to get interesting.

So read on, the fun's only just beginning ...

The long road to production

Now is as good a point as any to mention that theatre is not a democracy. There's a rigid hierarchy, for the simple reason that there isn't the time to sit around and discuss every-thing. Many playwrights, Pinter and Ayckbourn included, worked as actors before becoming dramatists. They under-stood the other side of the job.

The director's approach and the playwright's approach to the text are often markedly different. Some directors prefer their playwrights to be dead, and who can blame them?

Can I direct my own play?

Many artistic directors are reluctant to allow a playwright to direct their own play, and for justifiable reasons. Wisely, when Harold Pinter was directing his own plays he would ask the actors what the playwright was trying to communi-cate in a specific line or scene. He knew he must draw a line between the roles of writer and director.

A director brings distance to the play – a fresh outside eye.

Do I have any say in casting?

Once a director has been appointed, they will normally discuss casting with a casting director. You may be invited to auditions, you may not. It really is a courtesy rather than an obligation. Personally, I like to watch as many auditions as possible. Apart from anything else, it's a chance to see your play become flesh.

Some theatres may be more enthusiastic about a big name cast than others. Inevitably, it depends on budget. Don't take it personally if a part is offered only to be turned down by an actor, especially if the play is being performed outside London. Some actors are less willing to perform in regional theatres, for the simple reason that it takes them out of the casting loop, and means it's less likely that they'll be able to attend auditions for their next job after your production has come to an end.

It's tremendously flattering to think that an actor has taken the role because he likes your play. And chances are that's *precisely* why he took the part.

What is 'through-casting'?

It's sometimes cheaper for a theatre to cast actors for a whole season of plays, rather than for each specific play in turn. Sometimes it works, sometimes it doesn't. The adverse effect of this is the possibility that nobody is quite right for any of the parts they're playing. But it can be a necessary evil, and often makes larger-cast plays more affordable to mount.

First read-through

The read-through can be a real eye (and ear) opener. You've probably heard sections of your script in audition, but this may be the first time you've heard the play in its entirety. It can feel like a slow death.

Not all directors plunge straight into the script after the initial read-through. It all depends on the length of the rehearsal period. Have a chat with your director before rehearsals start. He will often have a clear idea of how he wants rehearsals to progress.

It's a good idea to space out your attendance days, and certainly allow for a couple of days later on in the rehearsal process. Even when I haven't been in rehearsal I have sometimes received a phone call asking me to have a look at specific sections of the script that might not be working. A playwright is never off duty!

Rehearsals

As a rule of thumb, a rehearsal period is often three to four weeks. Each day's rehearsal will probably run from ten in the morning to around five in the evening, with tea breaks and an hour for lunch. It doesn't take a mathematical genius to figure out that three to four weeks doesn't really allow much time to rehearse a play.

It's worthwhile re-familiarizing yourself with the script before rehearsals begin. We write in the moment, and it's sometimes phenomenally hard work trying to remember exactly *why* we wrote specific lines. Sometimes we never remember.

Re-writing in rehearsal

A script can change exponentially once you move into rehearsal, so don't think your work is over yet. Trust in the fact that the director and cast will work hard to bring your play to life, as slowly the production begins to take shape. Don't expect everything to fall into place immediately, it never does. Remember how long it took you to write the play in the first place? Well, there you go. The director and cast have embarked on a creative process that subtly mirrors that which you went through at your desk.

You will almost certainly find that sections of script don't work as you'd expected, or an actor finds it difficult to deliver a line and the director takes you to one side to ask if you can have a look at it. Don't make hasty decisions. Take a few minutes – go outside and mull it over. Remember, act in haste, repent at leisure. I have sometimes made a hasty re-write only to discover that it created problems elsewhere in the play. Then of course you have the added irritation of going back to re-write the re-write. All very frustrating and easily avoidable.

As well as getting additional notes from your director, you will undoubtedly find that your cast members have a number of thoughts about the play. Few people are as experienced at working from *inside* a play as your actors. Their feedback will often be very specific, focusing on their particular character's journey through the play – and their thoughts can be enlightening.

Early rehearsals can sometimes be frustrating for a writer. You want to hit the ground running. But just as you slowly found your way through the play as you began writing, so the actors need to slowly build up their characters. There can actually be a danger in peaking too early. Actors don't want to become stale. Don't forget, they'll be repeating the same lines night after night for the whole run of the play.

The input and feedback from the actors and production team may result in you looking at the play as if for the very first time. And this is never a bad thing. It is perhaps the moment when you are struck forcibly by the realization that if you dropped dead in the rehearsal room, it wouldn't matter – your script would go on (this may or may not be a comforting thought!).

Try to make yourself very available in the first week of rehearsals. This is the time when any problems with the script are most likely to be identified. From the third week the cast will usually be 'off book' with their lines learnt. For most actors it's a point of honour to learn the lines you have so diligently written for them with a degree of accuracy. If you find that your lines are being paraphrased, do mention this to your director. I have found myself in the agonizing position of sitting in the audience only to discover that one of the actors had gone entirely 'off piste' with the script.

I have heard a story of an actor who stumbled over his lines so frequently that the prompt actually received a review.

Do I get any say about the final look of my play – set, costumes, lighting design, etc., etc.?

Again, this all depends on your working relationship with the director. Strictly speaking, it's not all that important to keep the writer up to speed on the design aspects of the production, although as a courtesy it's good to keep the playwright in the loop.

Often a director will have a pre-existing relationship with a designer, who may design the set as well as the costumes for the production. The design process will usually begin before the play is cast.

Many theatres have their own construction workshops and are able to build sets on site. Smaller theatres may use outside firms of specialist set builders.

The designer will bring in a model box, with a scale model of the stage set. He or she will talk through any changes to the set in the course of the play, and will illustrate this by making the necessary alterations to the model box.

Where will I stay during rehearsal?

Many theatres will reimburse reasonable travel costs and will also pay for a writer's accommodation. In most cases the theatre will pay for you to stay in a hotel/guest house/ digs. If you're lucky enough to find that you've been put up in a hotel, it's worth pointing out that this doesn't include room service. On one memorable occasion, having failed to grasp this, I actually ended up owing the theatre money. But I had eaten well, so I didn't resent it.

Sometimes your choice of lodgings can itself be inspiration for future plays. I once stayed with a wonderfully eccentric landlady, a former student of the art critic and spy Anthony Blunt (a signed certificate on the wall attested to this fact). 'Do help yourself to anything from the fridge,' she cried as she took me on a whistle-stop tour of her house. I opened the fridge door only to discover a lone tin of Whiskas cat food on the shelf.

'I knew Terence Rattigan, the playwright,' she said. 'Gay of course.' She eyed me with a steely glare. 'Are you gay?' she demanded.

'Yes,' I replied.

She hurried off and left me to unpack. A few minutes later there was a knock at my door. My landlady stood outside, and beside her an actor who was also staying in the house, wearing nothing but a towel. It felt as though I was being presented with a sacrificial offering. I never stayed there again.

A brief guide to different theatre layouts

Proscenium Arch – perhaps the most familiar stage layout. The stage is contained within a picture frame.

Traverse – an envelope of playing space with the audience seated on two sides.

Black Box – many theatres have black box or studio spaces. As the name suggests, these performance spaces are often painted black and usually have the versatility to be set up in many different configurations.

Theatre-in-the-Round – rather like a traverse space, except that the audience surrounds the stage on all four sides. There are several purpose-built theatres-in-the-round in the UK.

Thrust Stage – basically a proscenium arch stage, but with an extending section of playing space which projects out into the auditorium.

Promenade – normally a site-specific performance space, where the cast follow the performance through a number of set scenes. This can take place in any number of 'found' spaces, from quarries to deserted hospitals. The only limit is the imagination of the creative team.

Inside the rehearsal room

Many theatres have their own in-house rehearsal spaces, many do not. I've rehearsed everywhere from Scout huts to Methodist halls. The important thing is that the space allows for an accurate representation of the stage space of the venue in which the play will ultimately be performed. From the first day of rehearsal the outline of the set will be marked out on the floor of the rehearsal room.

Passing over ownership of the play can be a truly liberating experience and there will inevitably be a period of readjustment, as the characters who – until now – have existed only in your head are made manifest in the rehearsal room.

The first day of rehearsals will begin with a 'meet and greet', where the playwright, director, cast, designer, lighting designer, stage management and representative members of each department (marketing, stage construction *et al.*) assemble. At this meeting you might well be asked to give a brief introduction to your play, to give background and context to the piece.

The first couple of days will probably be spent discussing the script at length. You might be asked to explain why you put pen to paper in the first place. You will have a captive and captivated audience, as the cast attempt to discover the motivation behind each and every line.

For a time you and your play are indivisible entities. Then a shift occurs; the cast have taken your thoughts on board and you are no longer needed to hold the hand of your fledgling play. It's a bit like snipping the umbilical cord. You're passing over the responsibility for your play to the capable hands of your director and actors. Your play is speaking for itself and no longer relies on you to be advocate on its behalf. This is as it should be.

As rehearsals progress you may quickly find you no longer have a specific function. At best you're a benign parent, at worst you're the spectre at the feast.

Tempting though it may be, never give notes to an actor. Any thoughts or observations you have should be channelled through the director. There's nothing worse for an actor than having a split focus in the rehearsal room and a director would be justifiably resentful if actors start turning to you for feedback and advice.

If I'm asked along to watch my play in rehearsal, what's expected of me?

A writer's responsibility shifts as rehearsals proceed. A director will often be grateful for your outside eye, a fresh perspective on the production. Again, don't lose sight of the fact that this is a collaborative process, but it's worth remembering that it's your spark of invention and creative vision that has led up to this point.

A theatre will normally pay for you to attend a specified number of rehearsals and this should be set out in the terms of the contract. To an extent it is up to you which rehearsals you attend.

Often rehearsals will throw up important questions about your play. Don't feel you have to bluff. You can't always remember why you wrote something. Be open to suggestions from the director and actors. Chances are they will only help you to strengthen and consolidate the drama of your play. But don't make changes just to please people. You can get to a situation where people start making suggestions just for the sake of it.

Sometimes there are important practical reasons why a director may ask you to look at a section of your script and make re-writes. Again, be open to suggestions, but never feel that you're being bullied into making a decision that seems wrong for the play. If you have a bone of contention, sit down and talk it through. It might simply be that the lines of communication have become crossed. But don't feel you've got to make any on-the-spot decisions and don't allow changes to be made to the script without your express consent. This is one of your rights and should be explicitly covered in the terms of the contract.

You may feel that you want to attend every single

rehearsal, to get a comprehensive understanding of the process. Be kind; give your director and actors a break. There are few things more intimidating than the constant presence of the writer, scribbling frantic notes. Apart from anything else, it looks as though you don't trust them. You become an unnerring corner-dweller, who is seen but not heard. Because there is an implicit, unspoken understanding that you are arbiter of what is the right and wrong way to handle your play, if you linger too long in rehearsal it can look as if you're checking up on proceedings. Even if you're not, it can often seem like you are.

There quickly comes a point when you start to feel like a spare wheel – and that's exactly as it should be. You've got some totemic value, but little more. You're handing your baby over to the day care of the rehearsal room. If you need to be there every step of the way, it's almost certainly because there are unresolved problems with the script.

It's extremely rare for a playwright to be banished from the rehearsal room – but it certainly has happened.

I can completely understand why some directors would prefer to work on scripts by dead playwrights. Even the most accommodating playwright is, territorially speaking, a potential threat. Again, it's all about status. The director, out of necessity, has to be the person in the rehearsal room with the highest status (although there are actors who would perhaps disagree). That is where the buck stops.

What do I do if the director asks for more substantial changes to the script?

It's often the first scraps of dialogue we write that we're most reluctant to lose. I've seen writers clinging desperately to speeches that clearly hold up the drama of their play. Try not to become too emotionally attached to the script. Allow a portion of your creative brain to oversee the process.

Cue-to-cue rehearsal

A cue-to-cue rehearsal is a necessarily fractured run of the play. The cast will be on call to give lines that are cues for sound or lighting effects, but it won't be a complete run of your play. Again, it's not necessary for you to sit in on the cue-to-cue, but it is interesting to see the technical aspects of the production slotting into place, especially if this is your first play.

Dress rehearsal

If you don't get much audience response during the dress rehearsal, don't despair! Remember, your *de facto* 'audience' is actually made up of theatre staff, and it's likely that they will already be familiar with your script – chances are they were there at the read-through on the first day of rehearsals. I have to say, it's particularly crushing if you've written a comedy and the tech crew sit in the auditorium watching the run in stony-faced silence. But don't base anything on this reaction – and certainly don't go off to make desperate revisions to your script. THIS IS NOT YOUR AUDIENCE. I repeat, THIS IS *NOT* YOUR AUDIENCE!

A play by any other name ...

Because a title is inextricably linked with the marketing of a play, I've waited until now to tackle this thorny issue. It really is one of those things that you either seem to get right first time, or spend forever trying to nail down. I once wrote a play that was originally called *The Death Of Constable Prout*. It might sound rather like the title of an Agatha Christie cast-off, but bear with me here. I still think my reasoning for the title was fairly sound. If the audience knew nothing else about the play, they would place fair odds on Constable Prout dying at some point. I thought it was a title that would help heighten tension. Instead, it just sat lumpenly on the page and nobody liked it but me.

In the end, a friend suggested 'Lam'. It was the name of the central character, it was also a dialect word for 'hit', and to make it even tidier, as the play was set in a butcher's shop, it had an additional resonance. So *Lam* it was. I can't tell you the number of times people have told me what a dud title it was. Ten years later, I still haven't been able to come up with a better alternative.

The title becomes your brand name.

'I hate plays with a seagull on the mantelpiece screaming "I'm the title, I'm the title, I'm the title".'

Noël Coward

How do I choose a play's title?

In 1997, following a complaint from a passer-by, a theatre in Florida was forced to change the title of an amateur production of *The Vagina Monologues*. Having renamed the play *The Hoohaa Monologues*, the theatre was obliged to revert to the original title by the playwright's American agents.

A title can conjure up the zeitgeist in a single word or phrase. Think of *Look Back in Anger* or *Shopping and Fucking*.

Sometimes there may be a phrase in the dialogue that has

a particular resonance and seems to sum up the essence of the play. However, be cautious when selecting your title. Sometimes a play can suffer from a stodgy title.

Think of all the titles that have sprung from the pages of the *Oxford Book of Quotations*. Often titles lose any trace of their original meaning. It's like saying your name over and over again. In moments of desperation I'll sit down with a pad and brainstorm titles. I'll frequently go round and round in circles until I hit upon a title I like. But just because I like it, who's to say anyone else will agree?

Audience members are often making a considerable cash investment in their night's entertainment. Apart from the tickets themselves, there's also the question of travel to the theatre, a meal out, programmes, etc., etc. You may have written a brilliant script, but your audience won't know this until they sit down in the theatre and the play begins.

Think again about your hook. A title is about as condensed as a hook can possibly be. You're taking an entire play and crystallizing it in only a few words.

I've always admired Michael Frayn enormously for having the guts to call a play *An Absolute Turkey*. It's handing potential ammunition to a critic on a golden platter: 'In the opening moments of the play it was clear that *An Absolute Turkey* was going to live up to its title ...'. Fortunately, Frayn's play was not an absolute turkey.

Remember, a pun that seemed hilarious the moment you put pen to paper is apt to pall in the months leading up to production.

Will I have to write 'blurb' for brochures?

It's not a bad idea to have a meeting with the marketing team to discuss their strategy for selling your play. Your production is one of many that they'll promote in the course of a year; it's your job to make sure it doesn't pass unnoticed. Do be prepared for the marketing department to ask you to contribute to advertising material for the play. It's certainly worth planning ahead with this. They will almost certainly be eager for you to distil the essential elements of your play into fifty or a hundred words of copy. You are the person best placed to market your work – and it's in your best interests to do so. After all, this is the first point of contact between your play and the paying public and you want to make a good impression.

How do I go about writing blurb?

Your play could be the next big thing, but unless an audience is enticed into the theatre to watch it, who's going to know? You're giving a potential audience member enough information to form their decision – whether or not to buy a ticket to your play. But don't feel you have to give everything away. It's a teaser that will give a *taste* of the play and fire the imagination.

Here's an example:

'Sondrine's customers are deserting her restaurant in the seedy backstreets of Paris, until Didier decides to vary the menu with choice cuts from the local zoo – and so the "Zookeeper's Supper Club" is formed. Ragout of penguin is one thing, but is Otto the Chimp an appetiser too far...?'

It's similar to the blurb you might read on the dust jacket of a novel.

If you feel that the poster image or copy is failing to communicate, then tell somebody. Believe me; it's easier to do this before the printing presses are set in motion, churning out thousands of posters.

Interviews

It's inevitable that you'll be called on to give some interviews, even if it's only for the local press. Often these will be carried out over the phone. Features writers are always looking for 'angles', so if you can think of anything, be sure to mention it.

I think my interview style, such as it is, could best be described as 'vanilla'. I'm so anxious not to offend anybody that I inevitably end up boring the interviewer to tears. Trust me, it's something I'm working to improve.

Previews

'Preview: That part of a theatre run which is not affected by bad reviews.'

Miles Kington

A preview is an opportunity to assess the play before the critics merrily sharpen their hatchets for press night. A road test, if you like. In a perfect world (and this isn't one), previews would be nothing more than an opportunity for the cast to gently ease into the run of the play – that verruca bath again. But life is rarely as simple as that.

A preview audience is aware that this is a production in flux, and adjustments may be made depending on their reactions. The truth is it's often very difficult to predict an audience's reaction to a play. Once previews have begun, you might find that you suddenly have more work to do – although there does come a point when, for your own sanity (and the sanity of your actors and director), you have to down tools and stop tinkering with your play. I have known actors who've bridled at the prospect of preview re-writes, but they are few and far between.

Although preview performances allow for modification of the script, in most cases it's unlikely that your play will receive anything more than a polish. But the cast should certainly be prepared for possible re-writes.

Previews provide the opportunity to hone the play as finely as possible before press night. This is particularly true of comedies. Sections of script that may have had actors falling about in rehearsal may meet with deathly silence. On the other hand, the discovery that a line that was not considered funny in rehearsal meets with gales of laughter in previews may lead to a certain amount of fine-tuning and recalibration. I don't think I could ever have imagined watching a play and thinking 'Don't laugh too loudly. Please, please …' But it's happened. I'd written a scene in a play – the penultimate scene before the end of the first act. I was pretty sure that the scene had comic potential, but I'd underestimated an audience's likely response. We were blessed with a particularly fine comic actor, who extracted every last ounce of mirth from the scene. The audience were laughing so much by the end of the scene that I knew for a fact that the following one, which took the audience into the interval, would inevitably be an anti-climax. Of course, by then it was too late to do anything. The previews simply didn't afford enough time to go away and re-write the act so we could bring down the curtain on the funnier of the two scenes. There was nothing we could do except grin and bear it.

Press night

Everything that can be fixed has been fixed. Your opening night audience has assembled. You have distributed good luck cards amongst the cast and crew. The Half is announced thirty-five minutes before the play begins, and marks the beginning of the countdown to 'curtain up'. It's time to leave the actors (there's nothing you can do for them now) and beat your path to your seat in the auditorium.

Then backstage, over the dressing room tannoys, comes the announcement: 'Beginners on stage, please.'

The auditorium lights dim and the first performance of your play begins.

'The last collaborator is your audience.'

Stephen Sondheim

Choose your seat wisely!

'I saw the play under adverse conditions. The curtains were up.'

Groucho Marx

The only time I've ever walked out of a theatre was on the press night of one of my own plays. As chance would have it, I'd been placed immediately behind a row of theatre critics. This is not a nice place to sit. I spent the rest of the performance in the foyer being plied with red wine by the marketing department. Nowadays, I always like to sit as far away from the stage as possible – ideally on the end of a row and close to an exit.

The performance begins and the performance ends. At this point some of the most fanatical reviewers will scuttle off into the night, to file their review in time for the following day's paper. This is a die-hard breed, whose commitment to the craft is beyond question. If they've dreamt up something nasty to write they might scuttle off even quicker. Playwrights are to reviewers what sun-baked corpses are to circling vultures.

You've taken months to write your play, the script has been fine-tuned through several drafts, you've had more critical responses to your work than you can shake a stick at. Surely your script is now review-proof?

Reviews

There can be very few professions where a critical evaluation of your work is lodged in such a public domain. After the euphoria of actually seeing your play on the stage and the nervous excitement of press night, nothing can ever quite prepare you for the shock to the system when reviews start appearing. I still shake with fear. It's like riding a roller coaster, but safer (physically, but not necessarily psychologically).

Writers can be grouped into two categories: those who claim never to read their reviews, and those who do. Or, to put it another way: those who lie, and those who do not.

Before the eighteenth century there was no critical tradition in British theatre. I always think this must have been a golden age. An audience either liked a play and responded with rapturous applause, or they loathed it and threw oranges at the performers. At no point until the end of the twentieth century did anyone apportion a star rating.

If your play is being performed in London, even in a fringe venue, you'd be extremely unlucky if no reviewer made the pilgrimage to your theatre. Even in the regions you may be lucky enough to be reviewed by a 'second stringer' for a national paper. It's easy to spot a critic in the audience. They're the ones with pads and pens.

Allow the dust to settle

Ask friends to read the reviews for you if it all gets too much, and see if they'll provide you with a digest of the good and bad bits. A number of writers wait until after the production has come to an end before leafing through the reviews. This is perhaps the sanest way of operating, although personally I can't ever imagine exercising so much self-control.

Critics will base their review on their own response to the play, and the reaction of their fellow theatregoers will rarely be taken into account. This may seem an obvious comment, but I merely mention it as a warning. Even if you get a standing ovation and half a dozen curtain calls, chances are it will not sway the critic one way or the other.

Reviewers will read all sorts of things into your play that were never intended. If you're wise, you'll take the praise and claim it as your own. If the comments are negative, take the moral high ground and ignore them.

Incidentally, it's always a mistake to enter into correspondence with critics (it gives them the impression they've won). I've seen writers reply to critics, and it's almost always a messy and undignified affair. Apart from anything else, it also shows the reviewer that the writer actually cares what they think. Rise above it. There are often times when you'll get hot under the collar, craving the right to reply. Sometimes reviewers will get something spectacularly wrong (nobody's perfect, even reviewers) – but even then, resist the urge to correct them.

With a new and unperformed play it's often hard to determine exactly where the fault lies. And if in doubt, blame the playwright! If this is coming across as embittered, it isn't intended to be. You win some, you lose some, it's as simple as that. If you're lucky, you may even sense a shifting tide. Many reviewers have modified their opinions of a playwright's oeuvre (although, as with variable-rate ISAs, this can go up and down). Remember, Harold Pinter received near-crippling reviews when *The Birthday Party* was first produced. Reviewers (though they may strongly disagree) are fallible as well. Don't take it too much to heart. I once sat two seats away from a notable theatre critic from a well-known broadsheet newspaper who kept waking himself up with his own snoring.

> 'I'll take any amount of criticism as long as it's unqualified praise.'
>
> *Noël Coward*

What happens if I get a bad review?

I once wrote a play about a post office. It was set on the Isles of Scilly shortly before the outbreak of the Second World War. Central to the play was the post office's new telegraph machine. This was grist to the mill for one critic, whose review was headed 'Telegraph Play Fails to Communicate'. Now, I have to admit I had a grudging admiration for that one, although I was left with the impression that the review had formed around the pun and not the other way around. A cynic could be forgiven for getting the impression that the reviewer arrives with a headline fully formed, and constructs their review accordingly:

'Telegraph Play Communicates Wonderfully' (less pithy!).

In years gone by, reviewers for the leading national newspapers had a vice-like grip on British theatre. Theatre managers hovered expectantly, ready to pounce on any glowing reviews that could be blown up and pasted to the walls of their theatres. But nowadays the influence of established newspaper critics is on the wane due to the preponderance of online blogs and social networking sites, which provide a more instantaneous – and in the age of the internet, a potentially more influential – response to a theatre production.

Post-show discussions

The only duty you may have left is to attend the theatre's post-show discussion. Most theatres will hold at least one post-show discussion, or talk-back session, during the run of a play. It's a chance for the audience to get 'up close and personal' with the cast and production team. Generally, this is a relaxed and lighthearted occasion, although sometimes the audience can ask bewildering questions that you can't possibly prepare for. I remember an audience member once criticizing the choice of a piece of music that had been used in the production. When I tried to explain the reasoning behind our inclusion of the music, the audience member got up and walked out. On another occasion, and with a different play, I was confronted by an audience member who swore blind that no man in 1942 would use the word 'fuck' in front of his wife. I was never going to win the argument.

By and large, post-show discussions will attract enthusiasts, who are deeply fascinated by the process that leads to the mounting of a new play.

Press packs

Do ask the marketing department which newspapers will be represented on press night. The box office should keep a record of which reviewers actually turned up.

After press night, you've effectively outlived your usefulness. The play no longer needs you; it has a life of its own. You'll often be sent a press pack, containing all the press reports of your play – which should include any published features as well as previews and reviews.

Hit or miss

> 'When I was good I was very, very good. And when I was bad, we folded.'
>
> *Neil Simon*

Sometimes a play can be a popular success in spite of largely negative feedback. You might be surprised to discover just how many plays that have entered into the popular canon of contemporary theatre were dismissed as complete failures when they were first performed. Conversely, there have been vast numbers of plays that were lauded to the skies, which you will never have heard of. I hope this offers solace, it was certainly intended to.

It's a sad truth, but sometimes things just don't work out the way you expect. It can actually come as a bit of a shock to discover that your play hasn't gone down as well as expected. You may have written a fantastic script, you may be blessed with a visionary director and an outstanding cast, but somehow the production fails to make waves. Unfortunately, it's a fact of life. If you can draw any vestigial trace of comfort from the thought that sometimes you can find yourself in an entirely opposite situation, then you've learnt a valuable lesson. There's often no rhyme or reason to it.

There's no doubt that a run of negative reviews can have an adverse reaction on ticket sales. This may well be more acute depending on where your play is being produced. Some theatres have built up such a loyal audience base that you could almost consider them review-proof. After all, going to see a badly reviewed play is better than not going to see a play at all.

What royalties do I get if my play is put on?

Don't wait expectantly for the royalties cheques to roll in, you'll only be disappointed. Because your commission will almost certainly have been paid to you as an advance against royalties, you will need to earn over a certain threshold before you see a penny. Sometimes I've ended up with a decent royalties cheque, sometimes I haven't.

Royalties will probably be paid within a month of your play closing, but don't depend on it. Anything good that happens is a bonus. Chances are your royalties won't be more than a few hundred pounds. It might be enough to pay for a holiday – but probably not very far away!

Will people publish a play that hasn't had a London run?

In the past it was difficult to get a play published that hadn't received a London run. Nowadays, publishers seem more enlightened in their choices.

We're fortunate in the UK that many play texts make it into print. Publication will normally be timed to coincide with the first production of a play. However, without a production of your play the chances of publication are small.

There can be few things more satisfying than unwrapping the published copy of your script and placing it on your bookshelf. Suddenly it feels like you belong. But don't expect widespread distribution unless the play has been a runaway success.

Proofs of your play

You may well be checking through the proofs of your script as the play goes into rehearsal. It is possible to get obsessive about this. There will inevitably come a point where you have to sign off the proofs regardless of the fact that you are still making changes to the script in rehearsal. As the publication of most play scripts will coincide with the first production of a play, so it is that the majority of scripts go to press without taking account of a number of changes and re-writes which will have been implemented by opening night. If a play proves to be successful, a playwright will often make further alterations to the script before any future reprint.

You will probably be paid a small sum for publication – and it *will* be a small sum. It's unlikely that you'd be paid more than a couple of hundred pounds. Think of it as a goodwill gesture. Take my advice – if it's your first play (or even if it isn't), blow this payment on something fun and trivial. Publication of your play is a badge of honour, so wear it with pride. Never expect to get rich off the back of a published play text, although sometimes a play text may end up on an exam syllabus and that may help to shift copies.

The up side to publication is the possibility of further productions of your play, particularly by amateur companies. Again, this probably won't earn you a fortune, but there's nothing nicer than the surprise arrival of a couple of hundred pounds for work you completed years ago. This is the closest many of us will ever get to a free lunch.

'Playwriting gets into your blood and you can't stop it. At least not until the producers or the public tell you to.'

T.S. Eliot

Become an optimistic pessimist

Audience reaction is difficult to predict. If it wasn't, every play would be a roaring success and would run for years. It's easy to imagine that your play will be such a success that you'll be propelled into the stratosphere. It is important to manage your expectations. That's the odd and disconcerting aspect of the job. One day it's up, the next it's down. Unfortunately, the downs often last significantly longer than the ups and that's part and parcel of a playwright's lot. Harness the creative energy that comes with any moment of profound gloom, then go away and write more.

Take heart in the knowledge that a meteoric rise isn't always beneficial to an emerging writer. Second plays are a bit like second novels and put unreasonable pressure on the playwright. Second plays are to playwrights what the albatross was to Coleridge's 'Ancient Mariner'.

If it's only about the destination and not the journey, then I think it's going to be a disappointing career. Those people with an innate propensity for self-flagellation are often drawn to playwriting like a moth to a flame. You will alternate between feelings of elation and despair – sometimes on a daily basis. In this respect, it really is a rather unique profession. I don't want to depress you. But if I don't depress you a *little bit*, I'm probably not giving you the most balanced view of the job.

What happens after the first production of my play?

It's tough trying to find a theatre willing to stage a second production of your play (unless, of course, the first production was phenomenally successful). Nowadays very few new plays make it into the West End, a trend that's likely to continue for the foreseeable future. The reason for this is entirely financial.

Even if your play is successful, don't expect to sit back and wait for the offers to roll in. You still need to continue managing your career and that means pursuing new avenues of work.

We all dream of overnight success. I've been dreaming of it for ten years now. I'm successful enough to keep writing, but not so successful that I can stop.

Have you ever heard of me? Well, there you go.

The rewards of playwriting aren't always financial. In fact, people rarely write plays for a fast buck and overnight celebrity. And that's a good thing. If you're looking for a 'don't get rich scheme', playwriting may very well fit the bill.

If you're reading this now in your penthouse suite, about to leave the hotel for the first night of the Broadway production of your play, then apologies. The next few lines may not be relevant to you. You may well be the exception that proves the rule.

Can I make a living as a playwright?

Even a relatively successful production of your first play offers no guarantee that you will find yourself inundated with work. I was once writing an article about playwriting and had started confidently with the opening line, 'It's still possible to make a living from playwriting.' A wise literary manager friend of mine suggested I change it to, 'It's still possible to *scrape* a living from playwriting.' It might seem a rather negative amendment, but it is an honest one.

I'm completely in awe of anyone who packs in their well-paid job to devote their time solely to writing. But what if it doesn't pay off? I think people often take the plunge because they feel that 'real life' is getting in the way of their creative vision – that they need to shut themselves away from the world in order to produce their best work. But generally my advice would be DON'T DO IT.

I sometimes miss that easy proximity to real life. I worked in a shop for a year before I gave up to write full time. It was a lovely shop, with staff I was very fond of – and day after day I was presented with a steady stream of unique characters coming through the door. I know writers who would pay cash up front to be given that raw material. The moment you step back to sit alone with your laptop, you're often depriving yourself of this tapestry of creative potential.

If possible (and if you feel you really need it), see if you can take a sabbatical. But it's always good to have a paid and secure job to return to – think of it as the life experience that will feed your writing. Giving up work to write full time can mean that you're cutting yourself off from the outside world. Take heart. You may well be getting far more mental stimulation than the deskbound playwright, sitting at home, twiddling their thumbs and waiting for inspiration to strike.

I had an inglorious interlude not long after I'd left university, cold calling for a company selling air filtration units. It was a gift for a writer. I had a boss who overused my name to such an extent it almost became a nervous tic:

'I tell you, Christopher, when you've been working for this company as long as I have, it takes it out of you, Christopher.'

When I finally gave up work one of my plays had been optioned and a further two had been commissioned. I was finding it increasingly difficult to juggle my job and my writing. It seemed a sensible time to take the plunge. But commissions can be few and far between and there is no such thing as long-term job security for a playwright.

For a brief period after university I would pop into my local Job Centre to sign on the dole. It wasn't that I didn't want to work, mind you. I made a game effort, asking every week if they'd had any playwriting jobs in. They never did.

How many commissions add up to a living wage?

So how many plays will you need to write a year in order to earn a living wage? Hold on to your hats – the answer may shock and depress in equal measure. To earn an *average* annual UK salary, you would need to be securing about two National Theatre commissions a year, or over three commissions from a smaller London producing theatre or regional theatre company.

If you didn't find the above paragraph shocking and depressing, you may well be the sort of person who laughs in the face of danger. Or you may briefly have slipped into a coma. Either way, re-read the above and allow it to sink in fully. *Now* are you shocked and depressed? Thought you might be. Most writers are. Like any club worth joining, there are always too many would-be members.

If you don't enjoy the hard slog of writing and re-writing a play, are you sure that the financial return will be great enough to make the whole experience truly worthwhile?

Don't over-commit

Be realistic about the number of commissions you can take on at any one time.

It's hard to reconcile the creative and the basely economic. On the one hand, you will want to earn a living wage. But if this means taking on more work than you can handle, the quality of the writing will almost inevitably suffer. And this is another reason why it is not always a sensible idea to give up your job to devote your time to playwriting.

Some writers are able to juggle several plays at the same time and you may be one of them. But then again, you may not. If every play you're writing progresses at a snail's pace, this could have serious consequences for your cash flow (and even the most committed playwrights need to eat).

Some people work well under pressure, but the gnawing fear that comes with the arrival of an electricity disconnection letter or notice of mortgage foreclosure may well get in the way of your creative thought processes.

Chances are you'd be better off juggling a regular job and writing in your time off until you're absolutely convinced that enough work is coming in to subsidize your new career. In the meantime, make the most of lunch breaks or your journey to and from work. Write when you get home from work – and work diligently over your weekends. If your soul cries out for you to write, you will find a way.

Meanwhile, keep in regular contact with your agent. Remember, it's in his or her best interests to keep you employed. As they say, 10 per cent of nothing is nothing.

Will it spell the end of your dream if you don't climb to the dizzy heights of playwriting fame?

If the answer is 'yes', I strongly suggest you consider some more attainable career goal. If you could sit at home, beating yourself repeatedly with a rock and get paid for it, sometimes it would seem a preferable job.

Some writers find that they're temperamentally unsuited to playwriting. Maybe their writing talents lie elsewhere. Perhaps they are in love with the idea of writing, rather than being in love with the act of writing. Although playwriting can be a trying process, it should still ultimately be an enjoyable one. If every day spent at your computer is a living nightmare you have to ask if you really are cut out for the job.

The process of creating a play will not necessarily become any easier with time – sometimes it can feel as though it's getting considerably tougher. If you can embrace the spirit of development with equanimity and still return to your desk with a spring in your step, then good for you.

It's not like producing an object on a production line. The process of working on each play will often change depending on the nature of the project, and the nature of the literary manager or director you will eventually be working with.

However, you will be equipped with certain tools that you may not have had when you wrote your first play, and these can go some way to preparing you for the challenges ahead.

Beware the green-eyed monster

It's normal to feel jealous of other writers. It is after all an extremely competitive market. I wish I could be magnanimous about the success of other writers, but I'm really not sure that I am. But while you sit at home seething with jealousy, it is possible to waste an awful lot of time that could be better spent writing. It's easy to wind up envying your fellow playwrights for all the wrong reasons, weighing your success against the success of others. At what point will you be happy?

It's easy for a playwright to get pigeonholed, especially if their rise has been meteoric. Becoming known as the dramatist who wrote 'that play' can be a considerable cross to bear. When it comes to playwriting as a career, better the marathon than the sprint.

What if my commissioned play is turned down?

A commissioned play can be turned down for any number of reasons. It's not always the fault of the writer.

Don't be downhearted. It can feel like a crushing blow – I know, I've experienced it myself. Although it feels like failure when an unsolicited script is rejected, that sensation is always worse after working for a year or more on a play you've been paid to write. It's very hard not to take it personally. You wake up in a cold sweat in the middle of the night thinking: 'What have I done? Did I just make the play a little bit worse with each successive draft?'

I have been in the unenviable position of having two completed scripts, neither of which were picked up by their commissioning theatres. With one of the commissions I'd just reached draft eight of the script. It was incredibly disappointing. In my mind I'd played through every second of the play in a theatre that was no longer going to stage it. I can remember the telephone conversation with the literary manager vividly. Her opening words were: 'I think we're going to have to stop.'

It felt as though we'd come so close and suddenly the play was dropped. We'd even discussed directors and possible casting. Ideally the literary manager/associate director and the artistic director will work as one, in perfect tandem. In reality, differences of opinion and artistic vision do naturally arise, and the buck really does stop with the artistic director. As the literary manager said to me on the phone, it feels like the end of a relationship. We were both working hard to keep the spark alive, but somehow it wasn't destined to end with wine and roses.

If a good play will not always make it into production, the hope would be that it will bring you to the attention of right-minded people who may well be in a position to see to it that your next play does make it into production. Nothing is ever wasted.

Many plays are not produced by the theatres that originally commissioned them. However, to sound a note of optimism, I can think of several plays that went on to be enormously successful after being passed over by the commissioning theatre.

Of course, if you're able to get another theatre interested in the rejected play there may be a financial up side to all this. As well as the commission (non-returnable) that you've already received, a theatre picking up the option to your play will also have to pay you. When one door closes another door often opens!

Stay alert for new ideas

Keep a file of newspaper cuttings. Even if you're grabbed by an idea you can't immediately do anything with, chances are it might lead to something at a later date. I've been going back through a file I probably haven't looked at in the past five years, and already I've discovered two or three treasured cuttings that have instantly suggested possibilities for dramatic development.

Stay in touch with your agent

Think of your agent as a deal broker rather than a commission seeker. A good agent goes to the theatre regularly and has her finger on the pulse of current dramatic trends. She may well have a strong sense of what could already be in development. It can be difficult knowing what's in the pipeline when you are sitting at home and feverishly bashing away at a computer keyboard.

Do talk to your agent. After all, that's what you pay them for and you have as much right to be properly represented as the biggest name on your agent's books. If you've got an idea for a commission, talk it over.

Any agent worth her salt would not dream of signing a

client that she feels unable to represent to her best ability. Even so, it is possible for a new and inexperienced play-wright to be overlooked. A good friend of mine rarely hears from her agent. Personally, I like to keep in regular contact with my agent, just to let her know I'm still alive and busily working away at my desk.

The myth of writer's block

Things don't always come easily. Try to avoid instantly attributing this to writer's block – that's defeatist. Actually, I still think writer's block is a luxury of exceedingly wealthy playwrights, who can comfortably afford not to work on a problematic script for a couple of months. It is possible to confuse writer's block and clinical depression. The cure for the former is to carry on writing. I'm afraid I can't help you with the latter.

Be kind to yourself. Don't immediately spring into self-flagellation mode if your writing isn't going well. You're not unique in experiencing these feelings. Most people can eventually find a way to work through it so try to tackle the problem head on. I won't tell you that the process necessar-ily speeds up over time. It all depends on the nature of the play. Sometimes it feels as though the script is writing itself, sometimes it feels like pulling teeth.

If you're finding it mind-crushingly difficult to write, move over to a different idea. After all, a change is as good as a rest. It's never a bad idea to have a 'pet project' – something that can grow slowly and run alongside your commissioned work. A commissioned work perhaps stands a greater chance of being produced – but take a punt.

Personally, I enjoy working kangaroo-like, hopping from project to project. The benefit of juggling several different ideas at the same time is obvious; it takes the pressure off any single project to succeed. If you have a short attention span (and if you do, I sympathize), it's always worth having a couple of ideas on the boil.

Conversely, don't bite off more than you can chew. Don't succumb to what I like to call 'Magpie syndrome': when a writer becomes interested in every new shiny idea that comes along to the detriment of the shiny idea he or she *should* be working on. It's like reverting to childhood, wanting to take another toy out of the toy box because you're bored with the toy you're already playing with.

As one door closes ...

Periodically the artistic team will change at a theatre and the creative vision of the company may well shift. It can be tremendously frustrating to build up a relationship, only to find that you're having to start a whole new relationship with the incoming literary manager or artistic director.

The up side to these seismic shifts is the fact that your contact may well open new doors when he settles into his next role after moving from one theatre to the next.

It can occasionally seem as though everything is in flux. But this can sometimes work to your advantage. While some literary managers may reject your work, who knows, you might be welcomed in with open arms by their successors. It really does work like this at times.

Tough times ahead?

Economically, times have been hard. Quite what the fallout will be for playwrights, at the moment we can only guess, although it's a fair bet that new writing will go through a fallow period. Theatres will naturally continue to commission new plays, but there may well be fewer commissions on offer. And theatres may also be less willing to commission writers without a proven track record. This may lead to a more conservative approach to commissioning. Obviously theatres will continue to invest in new talent, but perhaps with a greater sense of trepidation than was formerly the case. In the past a theatre might have taken a punt on an unknown and untested playwright even if this meant the possibility of a poor financial return. With a diminishing pot of commission money, it's hardly surprising if theatres push much of this money in the direction of sure-fire writers with a strong track record of successes. All commissioning theatres worth their salt will always be looking for the next Stoppard, Bond, Ravenhill, Prebble, etc.

Rest assured – no matter how difficult the economic climate, theatres are always on the lookout for good new plays. After all, a playwright's name can quickly become a bankable commodity.

> 'There must have been a point in my life when I had to choose between living and writing, and I chose writing.'
>
> *Alan Sillitoe*

Or, to put it another way:

> 'There is no more sombre enemy of good art than the pram in the hall.'
>
> *Cyril Connolly*

It's not enough to *want* to write plays. You have to *need* to write plays.

You can sometimes feel like Sisyphus pushing the boulder uphill. The question has got to be, where do you see yourself in five years' time? How successful do you need to be in order to make your career choice worthwhile?

How does anybody measure success? Being paid to do the job you love – surely that's a sign of success?

A lot of extremely good dramatists will perhaps never get the attention they deserve. It doesn't mean they're not successful – it all depends on your definition of the word 'success'.

Managing your career

The advantage that a playwright has over an actor is the ability to see holes opening up many months ahead. Obviously, to manage your career you need to find ways of filling these holes. If commissions are thin on the ground, go out and hunt down the next commission. A good writer will not just sit at home waiting for work to drop into his or her lap.

Networking is a term that carries with it many negative connotations. It seems rather unseemly to buttonhole the great and the good in the hope that this might lead to a commission, but it can really be a *quid pro quo* situation.

The non-cynical approach is always the best one. I try to keep in regular contact with people I've worked with – just an email or a phone call every now and then.

Talk to people; find out if they're looking to commission. You might even make some friends along the way.

Spreading the word

Although it is difficult to make a living solely from playwriting, there are a number of ways in which you can subsidize your income. Guest lecturing, for example. This is what business types might call a 'transferable skill'. Once you've got a few productions under your belt, it's surprising how many people will pay money to hear you talking about the craft of writing.

Actually, lecturing in creative writing can be an enlightening experience, which has a profound and beneficial impact on your own writing. It's a chance to stop and assess *why* you write the way you do.

Don't ever feel that lecturing is 'selling out'. Many writers supplement their income in this way. Just think – you may be the person who sparks the interest of one of your students, giving them the enthusiasm and encouragement to consider writing as a career.

Epilogue

> 'Writing has been to me like a bath from which I have risen feeling cleaner, healthier, and freer.'
>
> *Henrik Ibsen*

It's quite possible to stagger through life without ever contemplating writing a play and still end up happy and fulfilled. I only mention this because it seems that an insidious and sinister element would have us believe otherwise. 'Anyone Can Write' was the clarion call I heard from a theatre recently, enticing budding playwrights in off the streets. It chilled me to the marrow and brought to mind the

Child Catcher of *Chitty-Chitty-Bang-Bang* fame crying 'lollipops, and all free today!'

Don't get me wrong; I'm all in favour of the encouragement of emerging playwrights. But honesty is always the best policy and new writers deserve the truth, and there's the rub – how likely is it that their plays will ever make it to production? If they're going to be caught in endless 'development' cycles with little or no hope of a fully staged performance, this should always be made clear – otherwise a writer finds that one door is being opened only for another to be immediately slammed in his or her face. Without a production a play is never anything more than a blueprint; the beginning of a collaborative process that will eventually take the writer's words from 'page to stage'. It's a tantalizing glimpse of what might be. But development is not an end in its own right – it's merely a way of creating *theoretical* plays.

My hunch is this: it's always easier to get money to set up 'outreach' writing programmes than it is to get a production budget to stage a new play. I've seen some theatres set out to identify new playwrights suffused with near-missionary zeal and, I'll be honest, it leaves me feeling faintly queasy. It's a bit like *My Fair Lady* (I'm big on musical analogies) – Professor Higgins dragging Eliza off the streets and teaching her to 'talk proper', ultimately condemning her to life in a manmade purgatory between high society and Covent Garden flower market (nothing wrong with either, of course, it's the limbo in between I have a problem with). Is there ever really any need to drag potential playwrights in off the streets? Playwrights with real determination to forge a career in the theatre (and grimly face the privations that are part and parcel of the job) will drag *themselves* in. After all, let's be realistic, it's a privilege to become a playwright (and a privilege to remain one) and not an unassailable right. It's a massively overpopulated career, with very few dramatists able to scrape through on playwriting work alone. I'm certain that everybody has a play in them – but sometimes isn't that exactly where it should remain?

Theatre is not a matter of life and death

In 1735 the Irish actor Charles Macklin killed fellow actor Thomas Hallam by stabbing him in the eye with his walking cane. And what so affronted Mr Macklin that only the spilling of blood could pacify the man? An argument about a wig, that's what.

This is a story to illustrate the exception that proves the rule. Pretty gory stuff. It's easy to get so caught up in the moment that you lose all sense of proportion.

But unless you're doing something profoundly wrong, playwriting should never be a life-and-death sort of job. Breathe a sigh of relief that you're not a heart surgeon or world leader.

Parting thoughts

The other day I was walking along the street outside my house and discovered a postcard on the pavement in front of me:

'Thank you <u>so</u> much for the inspiration. Paul.'

The word 'so' had been underlined twice. The message raised many questions, but answered none. Who was Paul?

What was the inspiration he had been provided with? And, most bafflingly of all, why had the postcard been discarded? You're the writer – you work out the story!

Index

This index is in word-by-word alphabetical order. Play titles in italics are works by Christopher William Hill, unless otherwise stated.